The Cognitive Milieu

A Residential Treatment Approach for Adolescents

Richard Chalon Aiken MD, PhD
Lakeland Behavioral Health System

ISBN-10: 0692708979
ISBN-13: 978-0692708972

Go Ahead Publishing
www.goaheadpublishing.com

Acknowledgement

Many staff and many residents have contributed to the information in this book over the past twelve years and to each of them I owe gratitude. In particular, the cognitive milieu coordinators, Samson Latchison, Thomas J. Stanfield, Donna Scott, and Art Crist, with whom I shared an office for five years, contributed daily experiences represented herein. Appreciation is extended to Sherrita Allen who trained me as a milieu therapist to better understand the realities of that position. The creative foresight of Ray Luccasen, DrHSc, is recognized as originating the idea of the comprehensive cognitive approach and the resulting advantages enjoyed by our residents. Finally, the leadership and commitment of Nate Duncan, CEO, Lakeland Behavioral Health System, in assuring continuance of the very best of care for our patients and residents is gratefully acknowledged.

Richard Aiken MD, PhD
Medical Director
Lakeland Behavioral Health System
Springfield, Missouri
June, 2016

Prologue

This book was written for a most important but unsung group of therapists – those professionals who work all day with adolescents in a residential treatment setting. These therapists are often not titled as therapists per se, being assigned names such as "technician" or "direct care staff." We shall call them properly "milieu therapists," or even more formally "cognitive milieu therapists."

While the individual therapist may meet individually with the resident once or twice a week for an hour, perhaps with the resident and family for another hour, and with a group of residents once or twice a week, the other 165 hours or so are primarily the treatment domain of the milieu therapists.

The individual therapist introduces therapeutic concepts but these are practiced in the milieu. Therefore, a critical element for therapeutic progress is communication between the individual therapist and the rest of the Treatment Team, including the milieu therapist. This can be accomplished during staffings and through documentation such as the Master Treatment Plan with regular updates. Or through personal one-on-one contacts.

Given the importance of the milieu therapists, it is curious that there is no degree program or licensing for this individual. Typically, there are great responsibilities and expectations with little training. That was the main impetus for this book, a basic manual for the milieu therapist.

This need became particularly apparent with our residential program in which Cognitive Behavioral Therapy (CBT) is used comprehensively, across all treatment modalities including in the milieu. Over the more than dozen years since its implementation at Lakeland Behavioral Health System (LBHS) with thousands of residents, we have found this approach to be highly effective, providing the milieu therapist with an excellent tool to assist residents to advance in their treatment within a therapeutic cognitive milieu.

The idea of a "cognitive milieu" could apply to any setting, not just residential treatment. For example, we have applied it successfully in modified form to acute hospitalization at LBHS. The basic principles could be utilized also in group homes, schools, even family settings. We encourage the families of our residents to learn the basics of CBT techniques and bring the cognitive milieu into the home environment.

The main ingredients of the cognitive milieu are knowledge of CBT and the presence of a facilitator to help the participant recognize triggers and respond to them with reality-based logic rather than distorted conditioned responses.

Life is difficult. As Mark Twain once said: "*It's mind over matter, if you don't mind, it doesn't matter.*" Some situations, even faced with realistic true understanding are still difficult. If we can understand that and accept that fact as an integral part of the human condition, it is not so difficult. It's just life.

What we as therapists try to do is facilitate removal of *self-made* difficulties, those that exist because of negative unrealistic processing of our environment. Typically, these distortions are based on unpleasant memories of the past or fears of the future – not so much on what is happening now. Now can be difficult but manageable. The past, a useful concept that we can learn from, cannot be altered now – that's impossible; the future, also a useful concept that we can prepare for, cannot be dealt with now – that's impossible.

The milieu therapist helps the resident deal with the reality of now.

Table of Contents

Chapter 1

The Therapeutic Milieu

The Milieu is the Message

*R*esidential treatment offers the unique opportunity for constructing the environment to the therapeutic advantage of the residents. This environment consists not only of the formal therapies of the psychiatrist, psychologist, and social worker, but extends through all daily living experiences, what has been called "The Other 23 Hours[1]." At its best, the milieu is an orchestrated social system facilitating successful hands-on application of skills by the resident in response to triggers that previously led to maladaptive behaviors. The properly conducted milieu combines all interventions into a consistent and harmonious unity.

---

[1] Brendtro, L. K., Whittaker, J.K., & Trieschman, A.E. (1969). The Other 23 Hours: Child-Care Work with Emotionally Disturbed Children in a Therapeutic Milieu. Aldine Transaction; 1st Edition(PB) edition.

The following clinical example illustrates some of the elements of a good therapeutic milieu in the treatment of a patient who had been violent in treatment programs that used a more punitive approach:

"He was calm; his attention appeared to be arrested by his new situation ... the superintendent conducted him to his (room), and told him the circumstances on which his treatment would depend; that it was his wish to make every inhabitant in the house as comfortable as possible and that he sincerely hoped the patient's conduct would render it unnecessary for him to have recourse to coercion. The (patient) was sensible of the kindness of his treatment. He promised to restrain himself, and he so completely succeeded, that, during his stay, no coercive means were ever employed towards him. This case affords a striking example of the efficacy of (this) treatment. The patient was frequently very vociferous, and threatened his attendants, who in their defense were very desirous of restraining him. The superintendent on these occasions, went to his (room); and though the first sight of him seemed rather to increase the patient's irritation, yet after sitting some time quietly beside him, the violent excitement subsided, and he would listen with attention to the persuasions and arguments of his friendly visitor. After such conversations, the patient was generally

> *better for some days or a week; and in about four months he was discharged perfectly recovered."[2]*

This account is remarkable on several levels. First, it illustrates the use of a cognitive approach to the patient or resident that emphasizes self-control in a supportive milieu. Second, it is a clinical example from the eighteenth century of a "lunatic" who

> *"had been (previously) kept in chains, his clothes taken on and off by means of strings without removing the manacles."*

This treatment philosophy differed enormously from that of other "asylums" of the period where fear and intimidation were primary tools:

> *"strong chains were employed to hold the excited patients. These chains, fixed at different heights to the sides of stoves, have iron rings at the end, by means of which the arms or the legs of the patient are rendered completely immovable. Far from fearing that a painful impression will be produced on the patients by chains, they think, on the contrary, that this apparatus exerts a beneficial influence upon them; that it*

---

[2] Tuke, S. (1813) *The Retreat, an institution near York for insane persons* (p 147). W. Alexander Publisher, York.

> *intimidates, humbles them, and removes all*
> *desire to attempt to get rid of their*
> *fastenings.[3]"*

Certainly times have changed since the latter account of patient treatment; however, one could question whether or not there has been a substantial improvement in the approach to the resident since that indicated in the first account above, with the advantage of more than two hundred years of additional experience.

The intention of this book is to present a new model of residential treatment that is based on the use of cognitive behavioral therapy applied comprehensively across all modalities of treatment – most specifically in the therapeutic milieu.

Introduction

> *"From the moment they enter treatment*
> *(they) overwhelm us with symptomatic*
> *behavior. This behavior spurts into the life*
> *scene with great velocity and intensity.*
> *We are glad that it does. For this gives us*
> *the opportunity to work with it in a way*
> *which would be impossible if we had to*

---

[3] Tuke, D.H. (1882). *Chapters in the history of the insane in the British Isles* (p 140). Kegan Paul Trench and Company, London.

> *wait until the patient showed up (in the therapist's) office at '4 P.M.'* [4]

While the milieu is to have representative elements of outpatient lifestyle, it is more purposefully constructed. *"Milieu therapy"* is a phrase originally used by Bruno Bettelheim meant to imply the exposure of a resident to treatment by total environmental design. [5]

The residential therapeutic milieu is a short-term training program in effective living that overcomes previous less effective behavioral patterns. The resident not only learns useful social skills, he[6] *practices* them sufficiently in order to internalize or adopt these "coping" mechanisms as second nature. This prepares the resident for his "home" environment that may be more challenging and not substantially changed since he was admitted into residential treatment.

---

[4] Redl, F. & Wineman D. (1951) *Children who hate* (p 46). Free Press, Macmillan Publishing, Inc.

[5] Bettelheim, B. & Sylvester, E. (1948). *The therapeutic milieu*. American Journal of Orthopsychiatry, XVIII.

[6] The pronoun "he" will be used throughout this text as representative of a male or female.

> **Remember**:
>
> Behavioral change doesn't happen in the therapist's office; it happens in the resident's living environment.

A therapeutic milieu will *facilitate* proper behavioral choices and social growth.

Often the resident enters treatment thinking that it is he against the staff - that it is the intention of the staff to "brainwash" the resident and to change "who he is." This sets up a power struggle that can last throughout the stay on the unit. It is, therefore, very important from the beginning and periodically during the stay to emphasize that it is not the intention of the staff to change who the resident is, but merely to help the resident understand reality and provide training in thoughtfully dealing with it to his full advantage.

The therapeutic milieu might be quite foreign but welcome to a resident who comes from a non-therapeutic home milieu.[7] After a period of readjustment, the safety, structure, and support can be particularly reassuring and offer a context for substantial personal growth.

---

[7]Gralnick, A. (1987). The socially-oriented psychiatric hospital," *International Journal of Social Psychiatry* 33(3), 218 - 255.

Residential Care: What Good is it?

A number of studies have identified positive outcomes associated with residential care.[8] For example, a Canadian study of 40 children in residential care found that for most children, functioning was severely impaired at admission, moderately impaired at discharge, and normal at one and three years after discharge[9].

A study of children diagnosed with conduct disorder in residential care found the number of concerns expressed by caregivers decreased from admission to discharge, and six months, one year, and two years after discharge.[10]

A retrospective study of 200 children served at group homes in the Midwest found that, as adults, 70% had completed high school, 27% had some college or vocational

[8] Lloyd B. (2007) CWLA's position on residential care, *Residential Group Care quarterly*, 7(4).

[9] Blackman, M., Eustace, J., & Chowdhury, M. A. (1991) Adolescent residential treatment: A one to three year follow up. *Canadian Journal of Psychiatry* 36, 472 - 479.

[10] Day, D. M., Pal, A., & Goldberg, K. (1994) Assessing the post-residential functioning of latency-aged conduct disordered children. *Residential Treatment for Children and Youth*, 11, 45-61.

training, and only 14% were receiving public assistance[11] In a 23-year longitudinal study, Weiner and Kupermintz[12] found that 268 children initially placed in well-designed residential care settings functioned "well as young adults."

Characteristics of residential care that have been correlated with long-term positive outcomes include high levels of family involvement, supervision and support from caring adults, individualized treatment plans, positive peer influences, enforcement of strict codes of discipline, and a focus on building self-esteem.[13]

Prevalence of Emotional Disturbance in Youth

According to *Mental Health: A Report of the Surgeon General*, approximately 20% of the nation's youth are at risk for or have mental disorders.[14] Emotional disturbances

---

11 Alexander, G., & Huberty, T. J. (1993) *Caring for troubled children. The Villages follow up study*. Bloomington, IN: The Villages of Indiana Inc.

[12] Weiner, A., & Kupermintz, H. (2001) Facing adulthood alone: The long-term impact of family break-up and infant institutions: A longitudinal study. *British Journal of Social Work*, 31, 213–234.

[13] Curtis, P. A., Alexander, G., & Lunghofer, L. A. (2001). A literature review comparing outcomes of residential group care and therapeutic foster care. *Child & Adolescent Social Work Journal*, 18, 177-192.

[14] DHHS (U.S. Department of Health and Human Services, 1999), Mental Health: A Report of the Surgeon General.

affecting as many as one in five adolescents require treatment, and about half of those adolescents have significant functional impairment as a result, according to the National Institute of Mental Health[15]. This means that approximately four million youth who suffer from a mental health condition have significant impairments at home, at school, with peers, and in the community.

Some of these at-risk individuals exhibit "barrier behaviors," including extreme aggression, self-injury and property destruction that effectively bar some of them from meaningful integration with family, peers and at school.[16]

Children and adolescents without strong family or community support are at high risk of presenting in public systems other than mental health, including child welfare, juvenile justice, and special education systems, which do not treat mental health disorders as their primary mission.

---

[15] National Institute of Mental Health (2007). National Health Indicators Survey, *American Children: Key National Indicators of Well-Being,* See National Center for Health Statistics, Centers for Disease Control http://www.cdc.gov/nchs/ accesses through NIMH Website.

[16] Mccurdy, B. L., & Mcintyre, E. K. (2004). 'And what about residential...?' Re-conceptualizing residential treatment as a stop-gap service for youth with emotional and behavioral disorders. Behavioral Interventions *Behav. Intervent.,* 19(3), 137-158. doi:10.1002/bin.151

An estimated 50% of children and youth in the child welfare system have mental health problems; some 67% to 70% of youth in the juvenile justice system have a diagnosable mental health problem[17].

Characteristics of Residential Treatment

Residential treatment is a specific level of care distinguished by the services and setting. The definition of what constitutes residential care varies somewhat from state to state. We adopt the definition suggested by the National Association for Children's Behavioral Health and the National Association of Psychiatric Health Systems[18]:

- 24-hour therapeutically planned behavioral health intervention.

- Highly supervised and structured group living and active learning environment where distinct and individualized therapies and related services are provided.

---

[17] Huang, L., Stroul, B., Friedman, R., Mrazek, P., Friesen, B., Pires, S., & Mayberg, S. (2005). Transforming Mental Health Care for Children and Their Families. *American Psychologist*, 60(6), 615-627. doi:10.1037/0003-066x.60.6.615

[18] Final Report (2008). ABT Associates. *Characteristics of residential treatment.*

- Multidisciplinary team of clinical professionals (including psychiatrists, psychologists, social workers, nurses, special education teachers, activity therapists, milieu therapists and others).
- Diagnostic processes which address psychiatric, social, physical, and educational needs.
- Individualized assessment, treatment planning, and aftercare, involving the child, family, and community.

The purpose is to help each child master the adaptive skills necessary to return to and function successfully in the home environment and community.

Models of Residential Treatment

Orphanages and reformatories of the early nineteenth century were the predecessors of residential programs. The purpose of these institutions was to care for children and adolescents who could not be cared for by their family due to financial limitations, poor parenting practices, or disruptive/dangerous child behavior.

In the case of reformatories, obedience to a rigid structure was expected and aberrant behavior treated with corporal punishment, sometimes severe.

In the early twentieth century, there were the beginnings of a new interpretation of misbehavior that considered youth to have personality problems such as sociopathic personalities. For example, individual psychoanalytic therapy was extended to the in-patient setting, much longer term than typical for today. In psychodynamic theory, behaviors were given meaning from the unconscious.[19] The expectation was that these periodic interventions would lead to change in-between sessions. However, this model was found to be ineffective.[20]

Residential treatment as we know it today has been around for roughly 70 years.[21] There were some breakthroughs regarding the institutional setting as more "residential". Experiences in the milieu were recognized as life

[19] Ross, J.L. (1985) Principles of psychoanalytic hospital treatment, *Bulletin Menninger Clinic* 49(5), 409.

[20] Foltz, R. (2004). The Efficacy of Residential Treatment: An Overview of the Evidence. *Residential Treatment for Children & Youth*, 22(2), 1-19. doi:10.1300/j007v22n02_01

[21] Abramovitz, R. & Bloom, S.L. (2003). Creating sanctuary in residential treatment for Youth: From the "well-ordered asylum" to a "living-learning environment". *Psychiatric Quarterly*, 74(2), 119-135.

experiences within the group setting that could lead to life skill development. [22] Milieu therapists were seen as essential therapeutic professionals who could influence change through daily life opportunities[23]. While this point of view was indeed significant, long-term outcome post-discharge did not support long-term change[24].

Certainly one element missing in these earlier models was the inclusion of the family into the residential treatment process with life skills that could easily be adapted into the home environment post-discharge.

Today, the length of stay is much shorter and treatment models are more solution-focused. Two such models of treatment, providing scaffolding for milieu management, are the behavioral model and the cognitive model.

The behavioral approach uses positive and negative reinforcement to mold specific objectives and measurable

---

[22] Leichtman, M., (2006). Residential treatment of children and adolescents: Past, present, and future. *American Journal of Orthopsychiatry*, 76(3), 285-294.

[23] Maier, H.W. (2012) What's old is new: Fritz Redl's teaching reaches into the present. In W.C.Morse (Ed.) *Crisis intervention in residential treatment: The clinical innovations of Fritz Redl* (pp 15-27). New York, NY: Taylor & Francis.

[24] Hair, H.J. (2005) Outcomes for children and adolescents after residential treatment: A review of research from 1993 to 2003. *Journal of Child and Family Studies*, 14(4), 551-575.

behaviors. The more structure that is needed, the more frequent the reinforcements. This model lends itself well to treatment planning and outcomes study. A behavioral structure may be particularly useful for the aggressive conduct-disordered youth or those with limited cognition or slower emotional and social development. However, here symptoms are the target, rather than alleviating the underlying psychopathology. Chapter Two, *Behavioral Management*, considers some important aspects of the behavior modification approach.

The cognitive model allows for a more individualized healing of emotional disturbances so that the maladaptive behavioral symptoms are no longer necessary. This therapeutic approach is more likely to result in long-term improvement of the resident once discharged from the residential setting. It is also more complex than strictly behavioral techniques and requires training of the residential milieu therapist in Cognitive Behavioral Therapy (CBT), good working knowledge of each resident's psychopathology, and open communication with the treatment team. Chapter Three, *Cognitive Behavioral Therapy*, introduces basic concepts behind CBT.

In practice, some behavioral elements are necessary in any program, so that the behavioral and the cognitive are best combined into an integrated approach, what one might term the Cognitive Behavioral Model, taking advantage of the strengths of each component model.

The Comprehensive Cognitive Behavioral Model

A new model for residential treatment is introduced in this book, which we title "The Comprehensive Cognitive Behavioral Model." In this model, emphasis is placed on the clinical efficacy of Cognitive Behavioral Therapy across all disciplines including:

- Individual therapy
- Family therapy
- Recreational therapy
- Group therapy
- School
- Milieu therapy

We shall explain in detail how this model works and how it can be implemented in a residential setting in Chapter 6,

The Comprehensive Cognitive Behavioral Model. Our concentration will be on the last therapeutic modality in the above list, milieu therapy, which we shall call The Cognitive Milieu.

Behavioral Management

Principles of Behavior

*B*ehavior is anything a person does or says that can be directly or indirectly observed and measured. Behavior is sensed; that is, seen, heard, felt, touched, or smelled. Behavior is directly observed by noting it as it occurs, or indirectly by noting its result. Because behavior is observable and measurable, progress can occur and be documented over time.

The principles of behavior attempt to specify the relationships between the behavior and the specific conditions surrounding the behavior. There are events in the environment that occur before and after the behavior and these events can have a major impact on the behavior. To fully understand a behavior, it may be helpful for staff to remember the ABC pattern:

A ntecedent -	the events or conditions present in the environment before the behavior occurs
B ehavior -	what is done by a person
C onsequence	the outcomes or effects following a behavior

Antecedents can be simple or complex, recent or historical. A simple recent antecedent may be a staff request to get out of bed in the morning while a more complex historical antecedent may be cumulative psychological insults during the day in a clinically depressed individual.

The events in the environment that follow a behavior can be pleasant (reinforcing), unpleasant (non-reinforcing), or neutral. Reinforcing events following a behavior increase the chances that the same behavior will occur again in the future. Non-reinforcing events decrease the likelihood that the behavior will occur again. Thus, analyzing what occurs right after a behavior allows staff to analyze the behavior and predict its future course.

Consequences can be natural or applied. Natural consequences are the typical outcomes of a behavior without any intentional human intervention. Applied consequences for behavior are outcomes that are deliberately arranged. Applied consequences work best when they are logically related to the behavior. For example, the logical consequence for a resident who repeatedly does not awaken on schedule in the morning is for the resident to go to sleep at an earlier time.

> **Remember:**
>
> Consequences, when appropriate and correctly administered, are a good model of what happens in "real life."

Teaching the ABCs

How does staff help change behavior? By changing the antecedents, the consequences, or both. Staff will use discipline and positive reinforcement to increase the appropriate behaviors, while decreasing the inappropriate behaviors.

Punishment

To punish means to penalize, to cause pain, loss, or suffering for a wrongdoing. Punishment refers to the presentation or removal of an event that reduces the frequency of a response. In most cases, punishment is not effective when working with residents who have a history of being neglected, abused, or who are seriously emotionally disturbed.

There are many potential complications in the use of punishment:

- Punishment trains youth what not to do rather than what to do. It does not teach appropriate behavior.
- Negative behavior may return in greater intensity when the punishment is lifted.
- Residents may become fearful and avoid or mistrust the punisher.
- Punishment leads to lying, cheating or hiding.
- Punishment may feed into existing poor self-images and self-abusive concepts.

Discipline

To discipline is to teach. The goal of discipline is to teach the resident self-control, not to punish through adult-imposed control. If staff intervenes with any intent other than to teach, they are not administering true discipline. All behavior is purposeful, and to discipline correctly requires the staff to separate the motive from the action. Once staff discover the motive or goal of the behavior, they can teach clients alternative ways of meeting their goals. Discipline allows staff to confront an inappropriate behavior, impose a meaningful related consequence, discuss how the behavior backfired, and teach a new behavior.

Discipline is a process that requires an interaction: it requires a teacher and a learner; it requires mutual effort. It requires positive motivation on the part of the adult and the child. Discipline is not something that can be done to someone. Discipline allows the staff to move into and past the specific behavior in the interaction. The therapeutic milieu provides staff with a rich environment allowing a variety of formats for teaching alternative behaviors. The professionally oriented staff member will learn to develop a broad range of disciplining interventions when freed from the burden of merely penalizing and focusing instead on the mission of teaching. Characteristics of discipline include:

- Discipline takes more time and requires more effort than punishment.
- Discipline requires a focus on the individual.
- Discipline cannot be forced.
- Discipline enhances a child's self-image.
- Discipline requires a positive, confident adult attitude.

The difference between punishment and discipline is illustrated in the following table.

PUNISHMENT	DISCIPLINE
Reactive intervention after problems occur	Proactive focus on preventing problems
Adult imposes arbitrary consequences	Natural or logical consequences discussed with resident
Obedience to authority figures taught	Respect for social responsibility taught
Control by external rule enforcement	Control by internal values

Case study: The foul line

Josh is an intelligent fifteen-year-old male with a depressive disorder, a history of physical abuse, and a poor self-esteem. Occasionally peers will make negative comments to him and he will over-react and become extremely verbally abusive. One such incident was during recreational therapy - a basketball game in which a peer, clearly superior in court skills, taunted Josh to shoot the basketball. Josh was influenced to take the shot before he was likely to make it; indeed, the shot fell well from the mark, to which the taunting peer responded with a large grin.

Josh: *"You ____; I'm gonna kick your _____"*

Josh continued to utter expletives while posturing aggressively.

A milieu therapist asked Josh if he could discuss this with him. Reluctantly, Josh agreed but continued with the abusive language.

Josh: *"What a bunch of _____ I have to live with!"*

Milieu Therapist: *"I know it can be challenging".*

The milieu therapist listened empathically until the anger subsided. Then the following conversation ensued.

Milieu Therapist: *"Josh, it's your responsibility to yourself and your team to play the best you can but do you think this behavior helps your team?"*

Josh: *"I'm not gonna let anybody treat me like that."*

Milieu Therapist: *"He was playing within the rules, you stopped play and were threatening; as a result, you will have to sit out the rest of the game this afternoon."*

Josh: *"Whatever!"*

The milieu therapist later that afternoon discussed with Josh his feelings about being "made fun of" and how this reminds him of his own general inadequacies. However, he recognizes that he was being even more abusive to the peer and not accepting his social responsibility of the team sport. They concluded that he was going to keep in the front of his mind the idea of being kind to others, an important concept to Josh, as a motivation for self-discipline when anger arises in similar circumstances of perceived personal insult.

Positive Reinforcement

The principle of positive reinforcement states that providing positive consequences immediately following a behavior will increase the likelihood that the behavior will occur again in the future. Positive consequences reinforce a behavior and make the behavior stronger. Positive reinforcement can occur with natural consequences or applied consequences and is used to increase or maintain appropriate behavior.

Staff is often confused by the difference between a reward and reinforcement. Reinforcement occurs when a consequence of a behavior results in that behavior increasing or maintaining its frequency. Therefore, the behavior is reinforced; it is made stronger and more resistant to decreasing in frequency because the individual desires the reinforcement and associates the behavior with the desired outcome. On the other hand, a reward is given by an observer to someone for having met some criterion established by the observer. Often the giver assumes the recipient will like the outcome when they do not. A reward is what you think will work; a reinforcer is what is proven to work.

Reinforcement is effective only if the reinforcer matches the individual's unique characteristics and needs. This requires knowledge of the resident's likes and dislikes. Reinforcers may be social events, money, stars or tokens, points, praise, games, movies, or TV - to name a few examples. Staff must also know what part of the reinforcement is reinforcing, i.e., is the reinforcer successful because of love for the object, sense of success and positive feelings about self, love of getting something peers are not, recognition, or just attention.

It is best, if appropriate and possible, to deliver the reinforcer immediately. Delayed gratification is difficult for individuals with behavioral problems. As the amount of time between the occurrence of the behavior and the delivery of the consequence increases, the effectiveness of the consequence in strengthening the behavior decreases. The resident may lose sight of the connection between the behavior targeted for the increase and the reinforcer if other behaviors occur before reinforcement.

If a particular reinforcer is used too much, it will lose its effectiveness. A multitude of reinforcers should be available so that environmental reinforcers do not become more appealing and more powerful than the "same old thing" given for a desired behavior. In addition, staff must be aware of and monitor how much of a reinforcer to use. When a resident is given too much of a good thing, satiation will occur. For example, one piece of candy may be reinforcing while a whole bag full would result in satiation. Or, 30 minutes of TV may be reinforcing, while 3 hours results in satiation.

Response Cost

Response cost means taking away a known positive reinforcer for a behavior that needs to be decreased. Response cost is different from punishment because it takes away something positive rather than adding something negative. The same conditions that impact the effectiveness of positive reinforcement also impact response cost: immediacy, choice of reinforcer to be removed, amount of reinforcer removed, and removing the reinforcer contingently. Contingency statements and time out are examples of response cost techniques.

Contingency statements are "if-then" statements. If the behavior occurs, then the consequence will follow. For example, there is a unit rule stating all residents are to line up on directive in preparation to go to the cafeteria for dinner; staff tells the residents that if they do not line up now, then a certain response cost will occur. Again, as for any consequence, the response cost should be related to the behavior. For example, if a resident refused to line up because he was watching TV, the cost should relate to TV, for example loss of TV privileges for the remainder of the evening.

After making a contingency statement staff may state something like "*It is your choice to make and I trust you to make the correct choice.*" And then walk away; do not allow the resident to lure you into a power struggle.

Time Away

Clients who escalate during a stimulating time of day, for example, might respond well to time away. Time away allows the resident a chance to calm himself. Time away can occur anywhere but best in the day area or in the patient's bedroom. It does not have to occur in a special place, like a seclusion room, although that is an option that the resident may wish to request. Time away should be about five minutes in length. While in time away, the resident is to remain calm; this means no conversations or disruptive behavior. Should the resident begin talking with staff or become verbally aggressive or physically destructive, additional time away is indicated.

Time away can be used when a resident begins to escalate. Begin by telling the resident to stop the behavior. If the resident stops, give him lots of praise, if he does not stop, assign time away. When assigning time away to a resident, do so in a non-punishing manner ("*It looks like you are having a really hard time calming down; please go to the day area for a five-minute time away to calm yourself*"). If the resident complies, give lots of praise; otherwise make a contingency statement: "*If you do not take time away now, then ...*" (such and such will happen). If the resident complies, give praise; if not, drop the time away, remove the privilege and end the interaction.

Power Struggles

A power struggle may occur when staff attempts to force a resident to do something he does not wish to do. Power struggles can be dangerous for residents and staff. They often result in learned helplessness and compensatory reactions. This is how power struggles occur:

- A stressful event occurs (frustration, failure) which activates the resident's irrational beliefs ("*nothing good ever happens to me*," or "adults are unfair").

- The negative thoughts determine and trigger the resident's feelings which in turn drive the inappropriate behavior.

- The resident's inappropriate behaviors (yelling, threatening, sarcasm, refusing to speak) incite staff. Staff not only pick up the resident's feelings, but frequently mirror the behaviors (yell back, threaten).

- The staff's negative reaction increases the resident's stress, escalating the conflict into a self-defeating power struggle. Although the resident may lose the battle (receives consequences), he wins the war (his irrational beliefs are reinforced).

Power struggles may be verbal or physical. They involve control: power struggles exercise direction over, dominate, regulate, command, and hold in check. Power struggles can occur when:

- Staff have controlling personalities.

- Staff believe children should be seen and not heard.

- Staff believe their job performance is contingent upon the resident's behavior.

- Staff place value/emphasis upon compliance and reward compliance over empowerment and assertiveness.

Refer to the table on the next page for "myth versus reality" in regard to issues relating to evolving power struggles. Too often staff measure their own ability or believe that management judges them on the basis of whether or not they can "get the resident to mind" them. They feel pressure to keep on schedule and have no program deviation. However, in reality, the objective is to provide the environment within which the resident can grow in his personal emotional and social abilities and to facilitate realistic thinking and good choices.

MYTH	REALITY
I make individuals choose appropriate behavior.	No one can make anyone do anything.
By setting limits, I put myself in the position as the enforcer of punishment.	By setting limits, you offer choices. The resident ultimately chooses the positive or negative consequence.
I am responsible for the client's behavior.	Staff are responsible for the structure which provides consequences for the resident's behavioral choices.
When setting a limit, I must strictly adhere and not deviate.	You must be flexible if you want your limit setting to succeed. Each client and each situation is different.
Staff who set limits successfully get others to listen to them.	Staff who set limits successfully listen carefully to the resident with whom they are interacting.

Here are some pointers on ways to avoid power struggles:

- Personalize expectations
    - It's more honest
    - It's harder to "fight" with a person than with a "rule"
    - Enables use of the relationship between the staff and resident
- State the expectation/request/rule only once
- Follow up only with questions
    - Is that reasonable?
    - Do you understand the instruction and the reason?
    - Why are you having trouble?
    - What can I do to help?
- Keep the focus on the resident's difficulty with self-control
    - Getting into power/control makes it staff's problem
    - Issue is not whether or not staff can make the resident do it, but why the resident won't or can't
- Be watchful of language
    - Avoid "yes you will"; "you need to", etc.
    - Do not appear threatening in any way

Planned Ignoring

People often say *"ignore it and it will go away"*- the essence of planned ignoring. Behavior might extinguish when there is no reinforcement whatsoever. Residents will not likely keep doing something that gets absolutely no reaction. When what we do fails to work in any way, we stop doing it. For example, residents throw temper tantrums if that works for them and will continue having them as long as it gets them what they want. If staff decides to take no notice of the tantrum and are able to ignore it, eventually the resident will discard the tantrum as a means of getting his way because it does not work.

Remember:

As residential staff, we are facilitators of appropriate effective behavior in the residents we serve. When they make incorrect choices, it does not mean that we "failed".

When ignoring a behavior, it is sometimes important for staff to focus upon something else in order to control their own emotions. Staff should not make eye contact with the resident; not smile at, speak to, or touch the resident. As soon as the inappropriate behavior stops, staff should praise the resident.

Because extinction of a behavior through planned ignoring can be a long process and does not teach the resident alternative appropriate behaviors, it is not a preferred approach but one that might be used with certain residents after other techniques appear to have failed.

A modification to planned ignoring might be termed "announced ignoring" in which staff states calmly "*I understand you are not doing very well right now, once you are calm we can talk*" and not engage further until the resident is calm. Once the resident is calm, describe the inappropriate behavior specifically and state an appropriate response to the situation. When the client responds appropriately in the future, be sure to acknowledge the change.

Caring Capacity

The development and maintenance of close personal relationships depend on the capacity to understand, appreciate, and communicate meaningfully with others.

Once this social skill is achieved, positive relationships may ensue. Let us examine, in turn, these three elements of effectively and positively relating to others: understanding, appreciating, and communicating.

To understand you must listen. If you want to establish a quick positive relationship with practically anyone, at least for the short term, listen to them with genuine interest and ask for their thoughts on areas of some importance to them. Everyone wants to be listened to. If you want to avoid a verbal argument with practically anyone, actively listen, whether or not you agree with them. Listening validates others.

Understanding what you are listening to can be more difficult. To relate to the thought process of another, it helps to know "where they are coming from" or the core belief from which they are basing their thinking. This may require some effort on your part. You very likely have the ability to comprehend their viewpoint, as long as your own thinking doesn't interfere, or your own emotions don't distort what you are hearing. Regardless of the depth of your understanding of the "facts" and logic of what is said, it is imperative to understand feelings.

Appreciation of another's feelings certainly is made easier if you can relate to their specific situation through similar experiences you have had, then perhaps recalling similar personal feelings that may closely "match" theirs. However, it is not necessary to have experienced a like event to appreciate what it might have been like – you can imagine it. Even if you find that you cannot possibly relate whatsoever to another's viewpoint, you may be able to relate to the emotions they are experiencing.

This *empathic* process is sealed once your understanding of another's thoughts and feelings are expressed to them effectively. Illustration of a similar or imagined situation paralleling theirs may be given, but it is the congruence of similar feelings you have had to theirs which bonds and comforts most. This is the definition of empathy: to understand another's experience and feelings accurately as well as to demonstrate that understanding. Positive relationships require empathy.

> *"Every behavior is a kind of communication. Because behavior does not have a counterpart (there is no anti-behavior), it is not possible not to communicate[25]".*

---

[25] Bateson, G. (1972). *Steps to an ecology of mind*. London.

Cognitive Behavioral Therapy

It's the Thought that Counts

ognitive Behavioral Therapy (CBT) is a form of psychotherapy that emphasizes the important role of thought in how we feel and what we do. It suggests that it is our thinking that causes us to feel and act the way we do. Therefore, if we are experiencing unwanted feelings and behaviors, it is important to identify the associated thinking and to learn how to replace this thinking with thoughts that lead to more desirable results. We shall use the following definition of CBT:

> *CBT is an active, brief form of therapy or therapeutic intervention that focuses on a person changing dysfunctional or irrational thoughts, leading to more positive emotions and behaviors.*

No one "makes" us happy or unhappy. We can think positively or negatively, our choice - the former is healthy, the latter unhealthy. Children and adolescents develop "cognitive schemata" that integrates experience into their most basic beliefs. These schemata develop early in life, become reinforced over time, and are consolidated by adulthood. It is the aim of CBT to uncover these schemata or core beliefs, examine them, and make any useful changes through an active involvement of resident and therapist.

Introduction

There are several approaches to CBT, but most have the following characteristics:

- CBT states that our thoughts cause our feelings and behaviors, not situations. We can change the way we think and therefore the way we feel and act regardless of the situation.

- CBT does not require as much time in therapy with a therapist because it depends on more active involvement of the individual through personal "homework" and experimentation. It is based on the here and now and does not require an understanding of "how you got there", although identification of "core beliefs" assists long-lasting growth.

- CBT uses Socratic dialogue in that no point of view is imposed upon the resident. However, the therapist is very active in asking questions that require the resident to think introspectively about his view of reality.

- CBT is reality based. The idea is that if we can understand a situation as it really is, rather than as viewed through distorted conditioned responses, we can better deal with it without undue negativity.

CBT has roots in psychoanalysis. In *Mourning and Melancholia*[26], Freud suggests that depression can occur from imaginary or perceived losses, and that self-critical aspects of the ego are responsible in part for depression. A big difference between psychoanalytic theory and CBT is that the former focuses on unconscious beliefs/thoughts and the latter on conscious beliefs/thoughts.

---

[26] Freud, Sigmund (1917). Trauer und melancholie" [Mourning and melancholia]. *Internationale Zeitschrift für Ärztliche Psychoanalyse*. 4 (6): 288–301.

Cognitive and Behavioral Therapies

Cognitive behavioral therapy combines two effective kinds of psychotherapy — cognitive therapy and behavioral therapy.

Behavioral therapy helps you weaken the connections between troublesome situations and your habitual reactions to them. It also teaches you how to calm your mind and body, so you can feel better, think more clearly, and make better decisions. Chapter Two detailed some aspects of this type of therapy.

Cognitive therapy teaches you how certain thinking patterns are causing your symptoms by giving you a distorted picture of what's going on in your life and resulting in negative feelings such as anxiety, sadness, or anger without basis in reality.

While "cognitive therapy" is used sometimes synonymously with "cognitive behavioral therapy", we shall adopt here the convention that our approach to the adolescent in residential care involves both classical principles of CBT outlined in brief in this chapter for individual therapy (detailed by, for example, Beck[27]) as well as certain behavioral principles outlined in Chapter Two. Application in the milieu of a combination of cognitive and behavioral approaches is discussed in Chapter Seven, *Inside the Cognitive Milieu*. CBT has been modified for use in group therapy[28] and family therapy[29].

Why CBT?

CBT has been studied more than any other psychotherapy and is the only evidence-based effective treatment for children and adolescents with a variety of emotional and behavioral disturbances including depression, anxiety, impulse control disorders, and conduct disorders. Many controlled research studies indicate its effectiveness in a variety of treatment settings including residential treatment.

---

[27] Beck, J. S. (1995). *Cognitive therapy: Basics and beyond*. New York: Guilford Press.

[28] Freeman et al. (1993) Group cognitive therapy with inpatients", in Wright, M. Thase, Beck, A., & Ludgate, J., ed. *Cognitive therapy with inpatients* (pp. 121–53). New York: Guilford Press.

[29] Bedrosian, R. C., & Bozicas, G. D. (1994). *Treating family of origin problems: A cognitive approach*. New York: Guilford Press.

Socratic Questioning

CBT has philosophic roots in the work of Socrates. As Aristotle summarized, "It was the practice of Socrates to ask questions but not to give answers". The story of Socrates is well known: he traveled through the city of Athens speaking with many notable citizens of the day and questioning their views. Exploration of their thinking often revealed uncertainties and inconsistencies.

A similar approach[30] [31]is used with CBT in that the individual needs to note and examine negative "self-talk" and logically examine these thoughts through a series of questions. A therapist can facilitate such thinking by such questions as:

- Why do you think that is right?
- What led you to think that?
- How did you come to that conclusion?
- Are those good enough reasons?
- What's another way to think about it?

---

[30] Overholser, J. C. (1993). "Elements of the Socratic method: II. Inductive reasoning". *Psychotherapy* 30: 75–85

[31] Overholser, J. C. (1994). "Elements of the Socratic method: III. Universal definitions". *Psychotherapy* 31 (2): 286–293

A taxonomy of Socratic questions, created by a school teacher, Richard Paul[32], provides some structure for the choice of questions according to the response of the student. One question's response will lead into another category of questioning not predetermined by the teacher/therapist. The role of the skilled teacher/facilitator is to keep the inquiry "train on track," but also to allow the students to "travel to a viable destination" of their own design. See the table on the next page for some example categories of probing questions that encourage thought exploration, taken from Paul.

---

[32] Paul, R., & Elder, L. (2002). *Critical thinking: Tools for taking charge of your professional and personal life*. Upper Saddle River, NJ: Financial Times/Prentice Hall.

Questions that Probe Reason and Evidence

QUESTIONS OF CLARIFICATION	QUESTIONS THAT PROBE ASSUMPTIONS	QUESTIONS THAT PROBE REASON AND EVIDENCE
What do you mean by that?	What are you assuming?	What would be an example?
What's your main point?	Is that usually the case? Why do you think that holds true here?	How do you know?
Let me see if I understand you; do you mean _____ or _____?	Are you sure? Are you afraid that is true or know it to be a fact?	Do you have any evidence for that?
Could you give me an example?	What else could we assume instead?	How did you come to that conclusion?

The CBT Model

A simple model of the human experience is the following: a trigger ("T"), usually from the external environment, results in an automatic thought ("AT"). That thought leads to an associated emotion ("E") that in turn can result in a behavioral response ("R"). Putting these elements together spells the acronym TATER, illustrated below:

 ### *T is for Trigger*
Triggers can be big or small,
    good or bad or in-between.

 ### *AT is for Automatic Thought*
This is the first thought that comes into your head.

 ### *E is for Emotion*
The way you feel follows the way you think.

 ### *R is for Response*
This is what actions you take, your behavior.

We have published a workbook titled *Think Again*[33] that utilizes this TATER acronym as a playful theme to teach the basic aspects of CBT to adolescents and young adults. The workbook can be used stand-alone, in individual or group therapy, and in the milieu. We have had considerable success with this workbook over a dozen years with thousands of adolescents.

Once the resident has a basic understanding of the principles, he can apply them in the milieu. When the resident experiences a disturbing emotion, he or the alert milieu therapist can initiate "doing a TATER". This can be a verbal process or the resident can complete the worksheet shown on the next page.

Here the TATER is modified once a negative emotion is noted. The resident then "thinks again" using the concepts of CBT until a more positive or acceptable emotion is achieved. Then a positive response based upon that improved emotion is noted. Residents can "do TATERs" throughout the day and share them with the milieu therapists or individual therapists, nursing staff, and psychiatrist.

---

[33] Aiken, R.C. (2016). *Think again*. Go Ahead Publishing.

A file of successful TATERs is kept by the resident to build upon. After sufficient training and demonstrated proficiency with using the TATER worksheets, the resident

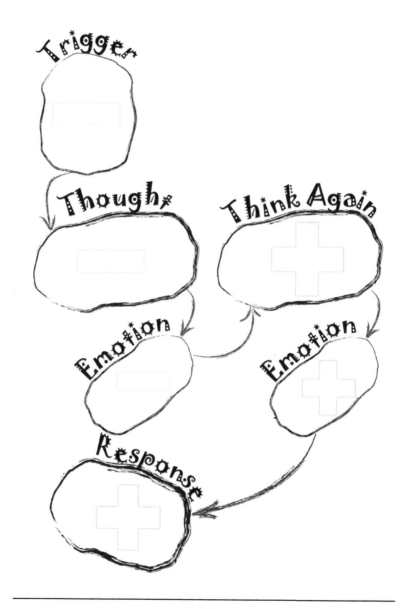

can mentally go through the TATER steps. Ultimately, this process becomes an integrated way of thinking without a formal TATER process.

The CBT-savvy individual will even "short circuit" this process by being aware of typical triggers and catch the process before the automatic thinking has led to emotional distress. The ideal state occurs after extensive analysis of many of these processes leading to an understanding of irrational *core beliefs* behind the trigger and the associated automatic thoughts so that they can be changed. If core beliefs are changed, the frequency of situations capable of triggering negative thoughts, feelings, and behavior decreases.

The CBT Brain Circuit

Speaking of circuits, there is a very logical medical correlate to the CBT model. Considering the brain as a "processing circuit," first perceptual information is received and is "processed" or "analyzed" in the temporal parietal lobe. It is then sent to the second branch, the "emotion circuit," located within the limbic structures, where the initial perception is given emotional meaning. Then the "signal" is sent to the third branch, the "relevance circuit," located in the prefrontal cortex. The response to the emotional content is determined there, whether to use CBT or act out, for example.

This "circuit" can be a handy - even if oversimplified - way of understanding the effect of certain mental disorders on the CBT model. For example, psychotic disorders distort perceptions - the first branch of the circuit; affective disorders and anxiety affect the second branch, and conduct disorder the third branch. Corresponding predominant neurotransmitters of these three regions are dopamine, serotonin, and acetylcholine, respectively. There are medications that specifically affect each of these neurotransmitters.

Trigger Happy

The first element of the TATER sequence is the trigger. As stated above, knowing when one is triggered is an important skill.

Triggers are very person dependent. Teens tend to have more social triggers while adults tend to have more emotional triggers. As indicated already, what triggers a person is related to how we "look" at the world - our core beliefs.

TATER Tales - Pull my Trigger

When we are born we see the world in simplistic direct terms. As we grow older and experience unpleasant situations, it is as if we begin to manufacture eye glasses through which we see the world. Depending upon how negative our experiences were, these glasses can really distort how we see reality. The idea behind CBT is to throw away the glasses and see things as they really are, to experience reality.   Reality can be dealt with using a rational process.

Case study: Stinkin' thinkin'

The scene is a room in which the resident, Courtney, is sitting reading a book. Another resident, Brittany, walks past and verbally insults Courtney in passing and keeps walking away. Courtney becomes visibly upset and is obviously considering her options – including whether to run after Brittany and respond aggressively. While in this triggered state, her milieu therapist notices her, sits down next to her and begins a conversation.

Milieu Therapist: *"Courtney are you okay?"* (No answer, just a glaring, angry look in Brittany's direction).

Milieu Therapist: *"What happened?"*

Courtney: (After a prolonged pause, turns away from the therapist and says), *"That b Brittany called me a b for no frickin' reason."* (Then turns around to inform the milieu therapist).
"You better keep her away from me or she's going to get what she deserves."

Milieu Therapist: *"Courtney, you know we have been working on your aggression in therapy using TATERs after a negative trigger. Could we work on that right now?"*

Courtney: (rolls her eyes) "If we don't, you'll probably keep me here longer, so what choice do I have?"

Milieu Therapist: "Well I don't know about the keeping you longer, but you always have a choice with your behavior and I appreciate your choosing to work on this. Okay, what was the trigger?"

Courtney: (hesitatingly) "That b calling me a b."

Milieu Therapist: "And what were your first thoughts?"

Courtney: "I don't know, I was mad, nobody can say that to me without getting their butts kicked. "

Milieu Therapist: "Do you know why you get so angry when someone calls you a name?"

Courtney: "I don't know … I'm getting tired of everyone always having an attitude with me. I'm tired of living like this, I need out of here."

Milieu Therapist: "Do you believe that other peers don't like you?"

Courtney: "Nobody likes me and I don't want them to like me so it works out fine."

Milieu Therapist: "Are you sure that others don't like you? What proof do you have?"

Courtney: (angrily) "Brittany just called me a b!"

Milieu Therapist: *"Do you think maybe Brittany is having a difficult time right now for some reason?"*

Courtney: *"That's her problem!"*

Milieu Therapist: *"Exactly. Is it necessary that you take on her problem?"*

Courtney: *(calmer, appears to get the point) "She should apologize."*

Analysis: In this case study, the astute milieu therapist is on-the-spot to turn a potentially dangerous situation into a learning experience. Courtney is probably too angry at the moment to sit down and work on a TATER worksheet but the milieu therapist essentially works through the TATER and Think Again process with Courtney.

The trigger is identified as the name calling, the automatic thought is *"nobody can say that to me,"* the emotion *"mad,"* and a possible response is *"getting their butts kicked."*

The milieu therapist, who apparently has some insight into Courtney's way of thinking, goes a little deeper than the apparent trigger of being called a name and explores what may well be one of Courtney's core beliefs that she is disliked or generally rejected by others. Then the milieu therapist challenges that belief and encourages Courtney to think again about the context of the remark made by Brittany. Courtney correctly identifies the fact that Brittany is responsible for the inappropriate remark and it need not be Courtney's problem.   In the end, Courtney is still unhappy but not acutely as angry as before and the resulting response is less likely to be violent.

Defense Mechanisms

One type of irrational basis for distorted thinking and resultant irrational behavior is the defense mechanism. Defense mechanisms are defensive behavior adjustments intended to protect oneself from emotional pain. It is important for staff to be aware of the various defense mechanisms and to learn to take into account the feelings behind the resident's words and actions. Some major types of defense mechanisms follow:

Denial

The ability to defend against painful feelings by not recognizing their sources. This defense mechanism is an attempt to refuse to face the facts. The resident who is angry that his parents did not come for a scheduled visit may deny that anger. The resident has learned it is not safe to be angry with his parents, therefore, he denies the anger, even though it is obvious to those around him.

Rationalization

A conscious effort to defend an action which has produced a feeling of guilt by coming up with a "good reason" for the behavior instead of facing the fact that it was wrong. Rationalization is a lot like making excuses, except that the client really believes what he is saying.

Projection

Projection is shifting the blame to someone or something else or attributing one's own feelings to another. Residents who have been hurt, or think they are going to be hurt, may blame someone else for their behavior. The client projects blame in order to protect himself. The resident's need to project blame will diminish as he begins to feel safe and comfortable. It is also important for the resident to know he is cared for as he is, not for what he does or does not do.

Displacement

Transferring an emotional reaction to a substitute when it cannot be directed toward the one who caused it. Displacement involves shifting negative feelings for one person or situation onto another person or situation. The resident who had a "bad day" at school, slams the door, upsets a jigsaw puzzle and starts a fight has displaced his anger. It is important to remember that the person who receives the resident's anger may not be the cause of their anger. It is useful to find the reason for the resident's anger, regardless of to whom the anger is directed.

Identification

Identification is an attempt to be like someone else. Identification has occurred when a shy resident who is fearful of tough boys becomes a bully. This resident attempts to become like the tough boys in order to protect himself. Identification has also occurred when a resident assumes positive aspects of staff via staff role modeling.

Reaction Formation

Reaction formation means to do the opposite of how one feels. Example: the resident who has been excited all week about his parents' upcoming visit and then yells and states he hates them when they arrive is protecting himself from possible rejection by attacking them.

Regression

Retreating from one's responsibilities and problems by an attempt to return to the comfort of earlier years by engaging in behaviors of those years (thumb sucking, rocking, baby talk). This can be a conscious decision to regress or unconscious. It is a common unconscious phenomenon with physical sickness or infirmity.

TATER Tales - Mashed TATER Tot

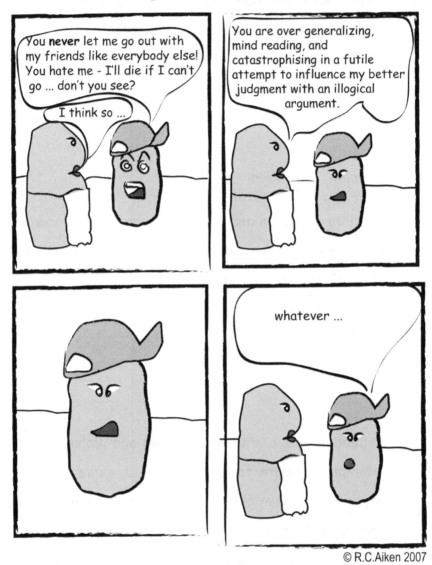

© R.C.Aiken 2007

Core Beliefs

As stated, not only does CBT practiced on a regular basis lead to better emotions and response outcomes, it can lead to an understanding of irrational core beliefs that once

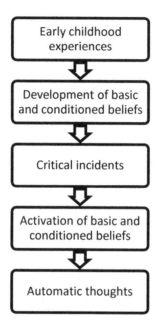

identified can be replaced with a healthier, more realistic understanding of oneself and one's relationship to the environment.

We begin very early in life, perhaps at birth or even before, having experiences that result in conditioned beliefs.

These experiences result in a schema of basic beliefs about our environment and how we should react to it.

If our experiences are particularly harsh, we might well develop a negative attitude about life. Particularly extraordinary circumstances such as physical or sexual abuse or neglect early in life can critically influence our thought structure.

By early adulthood many individuals will have established – by default, without a logical analysis – their core beliefs that will then be activated or triggered by external events into automatic thinking and conditioned responses.

Identification of the core beliefs with logical examination of their validity can alter these beliefs into a reality-based structure.

TATER Tales - Steamed Potatoes

© R.C.Aiken 2007

Psychopathology

Understanding Behavior through Classification and Description

*N*ot every resident has a significant mental disorder. Some residents will have distorted thinking which leads to poor choices of behavior but without a psychiatric diagnosis. Their conditioned responses, however, may correspondingly be antisocial, aggressive, and unacceptable to social settings, necessitating residential treatment.

Others may have mental disorders that substantially influence their emotional states and behavior. Regardless of their psychiatric diagnosis, each resident needs to follow the rules of the unit and participate in all offered therapies.

There will be occasional exceptions, but these will be ordered by the psychiatrist on a case-by-case basis. Mental disorder is not an excuse to break rules.

A good rule of thumb to keep in mind when defining a mental disorder is this: if the emotional signs and symptoms are sufficient to significantly and adversely impact the functioning of the individual, there may be a disorder present. For example, if a resident obsesses about a certain topic or has compulsions to do certain things, that would not lead to a diagnosis of Obsessive-Compulsive Disorder unless these obsessions and compulsions are so strong and frequent as to interfere with normal daily functioning.

Those who work in the therapeutic milieu need to understand what the patient's diagnosis tells them about their behavior. This helps to individualize a diagnosis-specific milieu management.

The behaviors and affects you observe and communicate to the rest of the Treatment Team will have a major impact on the diagnoses and Treatment Plan.

In this chapter we shall highlight signs and symptoms of various mental disorders that the residents we serve may have and indicate some appropriate interventions for each. The determination of the correct diagnosis is a fluid process, so information gained through daily familiarity of the resident can assist the diagnostician in updating the diagnosis, if indicated.

The categories we will examine include Major Depressive Disorder, Bipolar Disorder, Anxiety Disorders, Psychotic Disorders, Attention Deficit Disorder, Conduct Disorder, Oppositional Defiant Disorder, and Substance Abuse. As you read through this material, be aware that a single sign or symptom does not necessarily indicate that a mental health problem exists. However, it is a warning to observe the youth more closely and to document and communicate what you observe. A sign is a readily identifiable and objective behavior such as insomnia, vomiting, and tremor. A symptom is more subjective, such as irritability, anger, and inattention.

Causation of Mental Disorders

If we knew what caused the emergence of a mental disorder in an individual, we might better prophylactically avoid causal factors, and if already present, better irradiate the disorder.

Early historic conceptualizations of mental disorders invoked an association with evil. Treatments could be shunning or isolation of the affected individual - even execution.

Hippocrates (c 460 – c 370 BC), considered by some to be the father of Western medicine, allegedly stated that people should

"Let food be thy medicine and medicine thy food."

He separated the discipline of medicine from religion, believing and arguing that disease was not a punishment inflicted by the gods but rather the product of environmental factors, diet, and lifestyle. The therapeutic approach was based on "the healing power of nature" (*vis medicatrix naturae*)[34]. According to this doctrine, the body contains within itself the power to rebalance and heal. Only very recently has Western thought returned to holistic understanding of the patient in disease and health.

The "monoamine hypothesis [35] " is a more recent explanation for the existence of mental disorders that suggests causation associated with "chemical imbalances" of certain monoamine neurotransmitters. For example, abnormal levels of dopamine are noted in individuals with Schizophrenia (elevated levels) and Attention Deficit Disorder (lowered levels). Dysfunctions of the production of serotonin are implicated in clinical depression and anxiety disorders such as general anxiety disorder, obsessive-compulsive disorder, and post-traumatic disorder. However, while there is a correlation with abnormal concentrations of certain neurotransmitters in areas of the brain, this is no longer considered causal.

---

[34] Hiroshi, H. (1998) On vis medicatrix naturae and Hippocratic idea of physis. *Memoirs of School of Health Sciences*, Faculty of Medicine, Kanazawa University 22, 45-54.

[35] Hindmarch I (2002). Beyond the monoamine hypothesis: mechanisms, molecules and methods. *Eur Psychiatry*. 17 Suppl 3, 294–9.

While we still do not understand the etiology of mental illness, we do appreciate that there are many causal factors acting in a complex fashion. This is suggested, for example, by the discovery that many genes are involved as well as epigenetic factors. The epigenetic factors are influenced by environment and emotional stress.

Stress is governed in part by the excessive activity of the hypothalamic – pituitary – adrenal axis. Recent studies show that bacteria, including commensal, probiotic, and pathogenic bacteria in the gastrointestinal tract can activate neural pathways and central nervous system signaling systems involved with emotions and stress, the microbiota–gut–brain axis.

Chronic inflammation as a causal factor in a spectrum of mental disorders has been established recently. There is a rich interplay of metabolic, endocrine, and neurodegenerative factors as a result of the chronic inflammatory state.

Thus there is interplay between biologic factors, environmental factors, and stress.

Perspectives in Diagnostic Accuracy

The beginnings of a systematic classification of mental disorders has its roots at Washington University in St. Louis, the Feighner Criteria[36], a forerunner of the Diagnostic and Statistical Manual of Mental Disorders[37] (DSM). It is interesting and revealing that the impetus for establishing some objective description of mental disorders was from a research perspective. To do research on a group of individuals possessing some emotional problems requires that the group be identified using some criteria so that additional research or replication of research could be performed on similar individuals.

Thus the DSM series originally was not meant to be taken literally as the definition of mental disorders. There is nothing "statistical" about the arrival of the definitions of the disorders; the criteria are arrived at through an ad hoc consensus of a committee of psychiatrists.

---

[36] Feighner, J. P. (1972). Diagnostic Criteria for Use in Psychiatric Research. *Arch Gen Psychiatry Archives of General Psychiatry, 26*(1), 57. doi:10.1001/archpsyc.1972.01750190059011

[37] Diagnostic psychiatry originally led this author to a career in psychiatry with subsequent adult residency and child fellowship at Washington University.

> **Remember:**
>
> You should be aware of signs and symptoms without making any diagnoses yourself.

So there is no "gold standard" to guide the diagnostic process. This is important to note in that there is undoubtedly a spectrum of different symptomatic types for each named disorder. Therefore, keep this in mind when reading the following DSM descriptions of each disorder – these are not to be taken too literally.

Major Depressive Disorder

This is the most common disorder with which our youth will present. Although many will be situationally despondent about, for example, being away from home, we speak here of actual clinical depression with signs and symptoms which can include some of the following:

- feeling hopeless
- showing a loss of self-esteem
- persistently sad and crying
- withdrawing from others and activities

- having insomnia and/or sleep disturbance
- being irritable
- being persistently agitated
- significantly losing or gaining weight
- expressing fear
- feeling worthless
- wishing to harm oneself
- suicidal thinking (with or without plan)

Working with the depressed resident presents challenges. First and foremost is being aware of any acute exacerbations of depression that may lead to self-harm. If a good rapport has been developed with the resident, there is an increased likelihood he will come to you for help. Regardless, an offer should be made to assist the resident through difficult times. If the resident shares with you in confidence thoughts of serious self-harm or suicide, that is a "secret too big to keep" and should be reported to nursing, the individual therapist, or the psychiatrist.

Give extra encouragement to those depressed individuals who make a good positive effort. Be vigilant for decompensation with isolation and potential opportunities to harm themselves.

Clinically depressed residents may not want to participate in activities of the unit and may require extra encouragement to do so. Participation often will be a positive opportunity for them to "get out of their head" by focusing on things other than their negative thoughts.

Bipolar Disorder

Bipolar Disorder is the flip side of the Depressive Disorder, a much less prevalent affective disorder. It seems that it is considered by many as equivalent to "mood swings." In actuality that feature is only one of many comprising the definition.

> **Remember:**
>
> "Mood swings" alone does not a Bipolar Disorder make.

Furthermore, by "mood swings" many mean normal to sad or angry, whereas as a diagnostic element it really refers to a depressed state shifting to a manic state (or visa versa). Elements of this disorder may include:

- inflated self-esteem or grandiosity
- decreased need for sleep (e.g., feels rested after only 3 hours of sleep)
- more talkative than usual or pressure to keep talking
- flight of ideas or subjective experience that thoughts are racing
- attention is easily drawn to unimportant or irrelevant items
- increase in goal-directed activity or psychomotor agitation
- excessive involvement in pleasurable activities that have a high potential for painful consequences

The manic resident is less likely to follow unit rules, being impulsive with their own agenda. They may be quite engaging and humorous. Watch out for high-risk behavior, as often they are fearless and think they can do things that they cannot. They may be very talkative and demand your attention; give them frequent attention but of short duration. Communicate acute changes in "mood swings" to the rest of the Treatment Team.

Panic Disorder

If a tiger should suddenly jump out in front of your path, immediate profound physical changes would take place to prepare you to fight or to flee. This "flight or fight" response happens to some without the tiger participating. For those folk, this uncomfortable state can occur without any stimulus whatsoever. For others, imagined stimuli, such as perceived danger from an unstable unit environment or flashbacks could trigger an attack. Some of the following symptoms could be present during a panic attack:

Remember:

Youth can present in crisis because they are experiencing a physical, uncontrollable state called a panic attack.

- chest pains or shortness of breath
- sweating or skin flushing
- nausea
- pounding heart
- shaking or trembling

- fear or terror of dying, having a heart attack, or losing control
- dizziness
- loss of the ability to think clearly

Residents may use this classification of their mental state when they are not truly experiencing panic, only increased anxiety. Nonetheless, the highly anxious state can be met with reassurance; participation in an activity that refocuses their thinking on a neutral topic can help. Slow deep breathing, say four seconds of complete exhalation followed by a four second inhalation is usually effective.

Generalized Anxiety Disorder (GAD)

A person suffering from GAD will be chronically worried about life circumstances. For youth it has been likened to "always worried that they will get a spanking" (or the 21st century equivalent).

> **Remember:**
>
> Youth with GAD may fear you and avoid you; be supportive and allow them personal space.

It is normal for people to be concerned about certain situations, but some people worry excessively and uncontrollably. They feel restless and on edge and have trouble concentrating. Symptoms include:

- increased heartbeat
- muscle pain and tension
- nausea
- shortness of breath
- irritability

Complaints of anxiety are frequent and usually not associated with GAD. Anxiety is a useful life force that can be utilized for accomplishing tasks. It is like a two-edged sword in that one side can lead to "victory" and the other side can snap back and be injurious. The approach to a resident with anxiety complaints can be similar to that for panic described earlier

.

Medications used for anxiety are often abused, so be on the lookout for the drug-seeking resident (typically they will have a history of substance abuse).

Psychotic Disorder

There are several disorders that can have psychotic features associated with it, for example Major Depressive Disorder, Bipolar Disorder, Schizophrenia, etc. Overt perceptual hallucinations are often indicators that acute

care stabilization is indicated, but not in every case. The more common psychotic presentations seen on a residential unit are of a delusionary nature or thought disorder. A

Remember:

There is not much you can do to help delusions or thought disorders other than be calm, reassuring, and listen.

delusion is a "fixed false belief." Don't even think about trying to logically eliminate a delusion; it will not work. Thought disorders are not cognitive distortions due to intellectual inadequacies or developmental delays or conditioned beliefs - they are a result of a psychosis. The best way to deal with delusions and thought disorders is medication – nothing much else works very well. Listen to the resident without being judgmental.

In the great majority of cases, residents who say they are experiencing hallucinations of any modality are in fact not.

They may be experiencing illusions, confusing auditory hallucinations with strong negative thoughts, or they may be manipulating. Auditory hallucinations are rather rare in adolescents. Visual hallucinations are even rarer; those most often occur when a toxic substance is ingested (obviously including hallucinogens), or with infection, fever, or other organicity.

Residents who have been hospitalized or previously in various residential placements have been asked many times if they see or hear things that others cannot and sometimes they will adopt the symptoms they have been asked about to gain attention. Nevertheless, claims of hallucinations should be shared with the Treatment Team.

Attention Deficit Disorder (ADD)

Residents with ADD will "drive" *you* to distraction, too. They can be particularly difficult to direct as they are impulsive and inattentive, often hyperactive. However, keep in mind that not all ADD kids are "hyper" and not all "hyper" kids have ADD. The signs and symptoms of ADD are listed below. Note that most all kids exhibit most of these features; however, only the truly neurologically impaired cannot function well because of problems in these areas:

- being easily distracted
- having problems paying attention
- acting impulsively
- not paying close attention to details
- not staying focused
- not following through on instructions
- not finishing his or her work
- not being able to organize tasks and/or activities
- losing things
- fidgeting and squirming
- constantly running around and/or climbing
- having trouble working quietly
- talking too much

Such residents typically need additional cues to comply with unit rules. It may be required to have the resident look at you directly before issuing a request. It helps if the resident then repeats back the request, particularly if it has multiple parts.

Post-Traumatic Stress Disorder (PTSD)

PTSD is an anxiety disorder that can develop after exposure to a terrifying event or ordeal in which grave physical harm occurred or was threatened. Traumatic events that can trigger PTSD include violent personal assaults such as physical or sexual abuse. Many individuals with PTSD repeatedly re-experience the ordeal in the form of flashback episodes, memories, or nightmares, especially when they are exposed to events or objects reminiscent of the trauma. This can be particularly true if the individual is involved in therapy centering on the trauma. Symptoms include:

> **Remember:**
>
> Know the youth we serve: apparent defiance could stem from traumatic remembrances.

- persistent re-experiencing of a traumatic event through dreams, flashbacks
- appearing unable to be close to others
- sleep disturbance
- outbursts of anger
- being on guard or hypervigilant
- having an extreme startle response

Not everyone who has been abused or exposed to traumatic events has PTSD. Many claim to have this disorder for secondary gain, including manipulation. However, if a resident has this diagnosis, avoidance of a trigger for flashbacks should be part of the individualized care the resident receives. For example, if a resident has a history of neglect and has been traumatized by being locked in a room, the resident should not be secluded. If they have witnessed violence, care should be given to remove the resident from the proximity of physical aggression on the unit or a physical restraint.

Substance Abuse - Withdrawal

We will not cover here signs and symptoms of the actively substance-abusing person as it is expected that the residents we care for will not have access to substances unless the youth has exposure to street substances after a pass or outing. However, a youth who has been actively using may be admitted with subsequent withdrawal. Look for:

- nausea and vomiting
- tremors
- chills

- panic or anxiety

- restlessness

- confusion

- lethargy

- disorientation

- insomnia

> **Remember**:
>
> Withdrawal from certain substances can be a medical issue when severe, requiring medical attention.

Withdrawal, if severe, can be a life-threatening situation. If you spot signs and symptoms related to these situations, you should contact nursing, the unit supervisor or the provider for the unit to ensure that proper medical and supportive services are provided.

The resident may try to "get high" on medications prescribed to himself or others by "cheeking," then hoarding medications to overdose for maximum impact. They may try to "snort" various available substances including prescribed medications. Watch out for acute mental status changes, particularly heavy sedation, dizziness, or nausea.

CBT has shown to be effective for treating substance abuse disorders.[38]

Conduct Disorder and Oppositional Defiant Disorder

These diagnoses are less of an emotional nature as straight behavioral. Residents with these diagnoses are more likely to participate in physical aggression. They tend to be more manipulative and sneaky. They will instigate the unit at times without being a visible part of the disturbance.

The best treatment is a strong unit structure, well defined and consistently applied with no exceptions. The Behavioral Model is to be emphasized although the Cognitive Model is useful too; the core values for these residents may be unethical, immoral, and difficult to modify.

---

[38] Windsor, L. C., Jemal, A., & Alessi, E. J. (2015). Cognitive behavioral therapy: A meta-analysis of race and substance use outcomes. *Cultural Diversity and Ethnic Minority Psychology, 21*(2), 300-313. doi:10.1037/a0037929

Milieu staff should be very vigilant in monitoring these residents as they tend to be sneaky and clandestine in their misbehavior.

Nonsuicidal Self-injury

Nonsuicidal self-injury[39] (NSSI) refers to any premeditated, self-directed actions that lead to direct damage of body tissues[40]. These actions are exhibited in a variety of ways, for example, hitting or punching an object to inflict injury to self; cutting, scratching, or carving skin; interference with wound healing; and burning. The extreme forms of NSSI such as dismemberment, castration, and autoenucleation are quite rare.

Formally, NSSI requires that over the past year, the person has for at least five days engaged in self-injury with the anticipation that the injury will result in some bodily harm but without suicidal intent. Characteristics include:

---

[39] American Psychiatric Association. (2013). Nonsuicidal Self-injury. In Diagnostic and Statistical Manual of Mental Disorders (Fifth Edition ed.). Washington, DC: American Psychiatric Publishing Inc.

[40] Kerr, P., Muehlenkamp, J., & Turner, J. (2010, March-April). Nonsuicidal Self-Injury: A Review of Current Research for Family Medicine and Primary Care Physicians. 23(2), 240-259. doi:10.3122/jabfm.2010.02.090110

- The act is not socially acceptable.

- The act or its consequence can cause significant distress to the individual's daily life.

- The act is not taking place during psychotic episodes, delirium, substance intoxication, or substance withdrawal. It also cannot be explained by another medical condition.

- The individual engages in self-injury expecting:

  o to get relief from a negative emotion

  o to deal with a personal issue

  o to create a positive feeling

The self-injury is associated with one of the following:

- The individual experienced negative feelings right before committing the act.

- Right before self-injury, the individual was preoccupied with the planned act.

- The individual thinks a lot about self-injury even if the act does not take place.

There is a growing inclination toward an increasing prevalence of self-injury, particularly with teenagers and young adults[41], likely a socially influenced phenomenon.

Self-injury in adolescents typically consists of superficial scratches to the left forearm (for right-handed residents). When these injuries are more hidden, they are often more severe in nature.

My own theory concerning NSSI in adolescents is that it is a form of group identification. When asked why a resident is in treatment, a typical response might be "because I am a cutter." I think, too, that the act of self-injury does disrupt repetitive unpleasant thoughts and brings the resident into the moment in a dramatic way. Such individuals do not possess healthy alternatives to controlling or pausing their negative thoughts and find it difficult to focus on the present.

While as milieu therapists we do have to be concerned with self-injury, it is very seldom a life or death situation, and usually not a serious medical issue. In many instances it is a

---

[41] In-Albon, T., Ruf, C., & Schmid, M. (2013). Proposed Diagnostic Criteria for the DSM-5 of Nonsuicidal Self-Injury in Female Adolescents: Diagnostic and Clinical Correlates. Psychiatry Journal, 2013. doi:10.1155/2013/159208

form of manipulation, particularly if staff appear overly responsive.

It may also be a type of cry for help that catches the attention of staff and peers. If that is the case, there may be a portal for therapeutic advancement.

Residents may create these injuries using their fingernails; if so, the nails should be clipped and buffed smooth. Scratches can be made from nails and screws and fasteners found around the unit or school, so it is important to always be on the lookout for potential implements. Pencils are often utilized in this way and should be carefully monitored and collected after each use. Glass, sharp rocks, and various pieces of metal can be found outdoors in play areas and constant oversight is necessary.

Inevitably, it is very difficult to eliminate all potential objects that could be used for self-injury.

Insomnia

Insomnia is a sleep disorder that is characterized by difficulty falling asleep or staying asleep. Symptoms include:

- Difficulty falling asleep
- Waking up often during the night and having trouble going back to sleep
- Waking up too early in the morning
- Feeling tired upon waking

There are two types of insomnia, primary and secondary.

- Primary insomnia is not directly associated with any other health condition or problem.

- Secondary insomnia derives from some other problem such as a health condition such as pain or depression.

In 1979 a Gallup poll[42] found that only 5% of the surveyed population reported never experiencing a sleep problem. It

---

[42] Study of sleep habits (1979). Gallup Organization, Princeton N.J.

is the most frequent complaint of residents[43]. However, insomnia as a medical condition is different from occasional sleeplessness and time awake at night is usually grossly overestimated.

Nevertheless, it is important to keep the nighttime environment conducive to sleep. Minimization of light, noise, and extremes of temperature are important considerations.

If a resident does appear to have a chronic difficulty gaining and maintaining sleep, do report to nursing or other medical providers.

---

[43] Other than complaints of food and anticipation of discharge date.

Chapter

5

Behavioral Emergencies

"I was just angry"

*A*s discussed in Chapter 3, we all have core beliefs that govern our behavior. Any dysfunctional/ irrational belief once triggered, can lead to dysfunctional/ irrational behavior. When that behavior adversely impacts others, it becomes a larger problem - not just for the triggered individual but for others as well. Residents are more often admitted to residential care because of externalization of their negative feelings through unacceptable behavior than for the negativity itself.

When a new resident is asked *"Why are you here?"*, a typical response might be *"because of my anger"* rather than identifying with the real reason they are in treatment, namely their behavior once they are triggered to anger.

Residents often personify anger as if it were detached from their own ego. This personification extends to the rationale behind destructive offensive acts: *"I was just angry"* or *"he made me angry."*

Modification of dysfunctional/ irrational core beliefs is the best way to avoid negative behavior because the trigger itself is removed. Next best is to apply cognitive behavioral techniques just after a trigger in order to immediately re-think the situation and arrive at an acceptable emotional state. We can

> **Remember:**
>
> Rather than asking a resident why he misbehaved – impling there could be a logical reason – ask what they were thinking.

facilitate residents in these ways, as discussed in Chapter 3; but what about the resident who will not participate in cognitive behavioral techniques and is in an emotional crisis that may become a behavioral emergency? That is the topic of this chapter.

Working with an individual in an emotional crisis consists of two objectives: minimization of danger and seizing the opportunity for growth.

Giving Instructions Pre-Crisis

If a resident presents with oppositional and defiant behavior that is more problematic than their baseline, the savvy milieu therapist will astutely be on the lookout for triggers that further escalate the resident's enhanced irritability. Meanwhile, the milieu therapist can enhance compliance with instructions. There are several steps to giving clear, polite instructions:

- Get the resident's attention by moving closer, calling the resident's name and waiting to be acknowledged.
- Tell the resident exactly what you want done and how you want it done.
- Specify when you want it done.
- Keep your tone of voice firm but polite.

Case study: Giving Instructions

Milieu Therapist: (approaches resident) *"Good morning Joe. How are you?"*

Joe: *"Okay."*

Milieu Therapist: *"Joe, I know you are working on a higher point score; your room is pretty messy and that will not earn points. Please pick up your clothes and put them away now; then make your bed."*

Joe: (appearing disturbed) *"I will later!"*

Milieu Therapist: *"We are going to breakfast in 10 minutes, you won't have any free time to do your chores later this morning, so do them now and get those points."*

Joe: (reluctantly) *"Okay."*

Analysis: The milieu therapist is direct, explicitly telling the resident what to do and when. He further gives motivation and an explanation why now is the time the resident must comply with the directive.

Demonstrating a Skill Pre-Crisis

Remember:

It is your responsibility as staff to make certain that the residents know what you want them to do and how to do it.

Often residents fail to do something not because they won't but because they don't know how. When giving a resident an instruction, be sure he is capable of completing the task. The steps in teaching desired behaviors are as follows:

- Identify the skill to be taught.

- Break the skill down into a sequence of steps.

- Physically demonstrate each step to the resident.

- Have the resident practice each step.

- Comment on the resident's performance, reinforce effort, and make corrections without being critical.

- Monitor the client's performance until the client can perform the skill alone.

Case study: Demonstrating a Skill

Milieu Therapist*: "Hey Joe, did you make your bed?"*

Joe: *"No."*

Milieu Therapist*: "Why not?"*

Joe: *"Every time I do, I still don't get any points, so why bother?"*

Milieu Therapist*:* (motions toward Joe to follow him into Joe's room) *"Do you know how we want you to make your bed?"*

Joe: *"Not really."*

Milieu Therapist: (takes the bedding off and begins with the base sheet, showing Joe how to tuck in the ends; then undoes the tuck and has Joe do it). *"That's it, you've got it!"* (The milieu therapist teaches each subsequent step until the bed is made).

Joe: (showing a degree of interest and accomplishment) *"Thanks."*

Giving Directives

A directive is an important communication tool that starts or stops a behavior. It is more direct than merely giving an instruction. Directives are effective when you sound and look like you mean what you say and follow through with the appropriate consequence for non-compliance. However, when you have to repeat a directive, keep it from becoming a confrontation.

There are several steps to giving effective directives:

- Get the resident's attention by going to him or having the resident come to you.

- Establish eye contact. It may help to say the resident's name, pause, and then repeat his name until he looks at you.

- Speak in simple specifics. While keeping eye contact, state your directive. For example, "*It's time to pick up your things now.*" Never ask a question unless you will accept a "*Yes*" or "*No*". Never lecture or make negative comments when stating a directive.

- Use an assertive, firm but neutral tone of voice.

- Praise the resident as soon as any attempts are made to comply.

Correct: *"Johnny, put your gym clothes on now."* (Johnny puts on clothes) *"Good job."*

Incorrect: *"Would you get dressed?"* (Johnny slowly puts on shorts) *"Hurry up, if you'd gotten dressed sooner you could be playing with your friends now. Next time listen to me when I tell you something."*

Crisis as Danger or Opportunity

 The word "crisis" in Mandarin Chinese consists of two syllables. The first syllable is the character for "danger"; the second is the syllable for "incipient moment" so a literal translation of the two characters might be the "incipient moment of danger." However, interestingly, this second character when combined with the character for "occasion" makes the word "opportunity." Certainly from a psychological standpoint, an emotional crisis is potentially dangerous but certainly offers more of a chance for change than complacency.

Dynamic Model of an Emotional Crisis

Consider the figure below, which is intended to represent the time course of a generic emotional crisis. Plotted on the ordinate is a measure of stress level and on the abscissa time. The situation begins with a trigger, originating either internally or externally. As time continues, it may happen that the stress level continues to increase in the escalation phase, comes to a maximum resolution, and then gradually recovers to baseline. Each phase is illustrated on the figure.

> **Remember:**
>
> The idea is for the resident to be continually mindful of the cognitive behavioral model to problem solving.

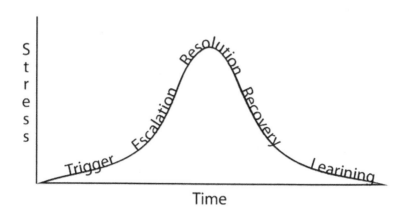

The apex represents the point beyond which the crisis is de-escalating or resolving. This point of maximum stress may represent an inflection point brought about by dealing successfully with the stress, with or without outside intervention. The crisis may have been successfully managed by the stressed individual using positive coping skills leading to a better understanding of triggers and dysfunctional thinking.

Or the point of maximum stress might represent the point of maximum danger where the individual has acted out — possibly hurting self or others or destroying property. This assumes that danger of harm to self and others is directly proportional to the stress level.

Recovery is still a potential time interval for re-escalation and may best be accomplished in silence, perhaps in the patient's room or in a designated quiet time away location.

Once the resident has resolved and after a recovery period, there is an excellent opportunity to review the incident while the thoughts and feelings are still fresh in the mind, using CBT.

So there are several phases to any crisis: the trigger, escalation, maximum stress, resolution, followed by recovery and return to baseline.

Other Crisis Models

The figure above assumes a Gaussian type of time course but many other dynamics are possible depending upon the person and the situation.

As examples, Figure a, below, is representative of the person who "bottles up" stress until a relatively minor trigger leads rather abruptly to the point of maximum stress; in the example, shown, the resolution evolves slowly. Figure b indicates "quick on the trigger" behavior,

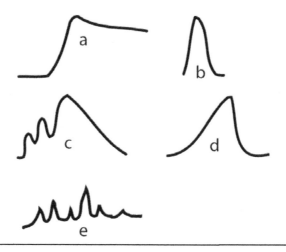

where a trigger leads rather immediately to a point of maximum stress and resolves relatively quickly as well. Figure c would correspond to a situation where an individual experiences a series of local stress maxima that partially resolve but crescendos to a larger overall maximum. Figure d shows an incident that escalates in a typical manner but resolves quickly. Figure e represents a resident who is easily triggered and escalates repeatedly but without major incident.

There are many more possible profiles of trigger, escalation, and de-escalation phases. Some residents have a characteristic pattern that once learned by the milieu therapist would assist with crisis management.

Opportunity, Cognition, and Behavior

Just as there is a direct relation between stress and likelihood of acting out, there is an inverse relationship of stress to cognitive capacity, shown on the figure to the left where stress level from baseline is indicated on the top Gaussian curve, and Cognition is shown on the bottom inverted Gaussian curve. This is why once a resident has become sufficiently stressed, he is less likely to be de-escalated using cognition and logic.

However, just after a trigger can be an excellent opportunity to use CBT, while the resident has an active need for a coping skill. There is another window of opportunity immediately following recovery of the crisis, as mentioned above.

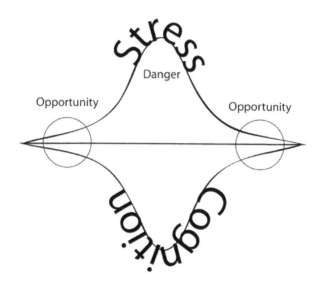

So what alternatives exist to cognitive therapy as the crisis escalates?

De-escalation

If the opportunity to use psychotherapy - for example, of the cognitive behavioral type has passed, either because of the high-stress diminished cognitive capacity of the resident or the refusal otherwise of the resident to engage, the objective simplifies to seeking a safe outcome in which no one is physically injured.

> **Remember:**
>
> One way of dealing with anger is delay.

The primary tool that the milieu therapist can offer is active listening. Most angered individuals want to be heard and understood. Offering that alone can defuse a situation, eventually. Active listening involves eye contact - but not staring down on the stressed person - that can escalate the situation. Nodding of your head to affirm you hear what they are saying is helpful (you do not have to actually agree with what they are saying; seldom will that be the case).

First of all, realize that de-escalating someone is a learned skill. Unless you have some training and some successful encounters, it will not come naturally.

Position yourself so that your eyes are basically at the same level as their eyes or below, without hovering above them appearing to subordinate them. Do not get too close to them - for your safety but also to give them space enough to move without feeling caged or trapped. If they are on a locked unit, allow them, within limits, to move about the unit. Do not require them to go to "time-out" or go to any particular place, although it is okay to suggest this for their own comfort and privacy. Generally, it is best to isolate them from intrusions, so if they are in the middle of the milieu, say history class, going to a more private location (in view of other staff) is preferred. If the resident will not leave history class, have the rest of the class leave the room, isolating the resident.

Do not touch them. An escalated person is likely to consider touch as a control maneuver, as physical aggression, and may respond with physical aggression.

Do not argue with them. Answering simple questions with direct simple neutral answers is okay, but generally listen rather than talk. Never even attempt to answer an abusive question (for example, "*Why are you such an asshole?*").

Show a degree of empathy toward their feelings (not their behavior) if you can do this without saying much - remember you are in the listening mode and anything you say can and will be used against you.

Give them time. We all have schedules, including you, the resident, and the unit, but these are not as important as safely de-escalating the resident.

Remember:

Time and space are the most important elements of de-escalation.

Staff must realize that their own behavior directly affects the way the resident behaves. Staff must remain as calm as possible. As it is a goal to teach residents self-control, staff needs to be the model of self-control and demonstrate this by the use of a calm voice, empathetic statements, respect of the resident's personal space, and by exhibiting great patience.

Residents may display a wide range of crisis behaviors. They may become passive, withdrawn, silent, and lethargic. Or they may be non-compliant and argue, complain, and swear. They may even make threats, damage property, or become assaultive emotionally, physically, or even sexually.

Many crisis episodes are predictable and, therefore, preventable. Staff must know their residents and learn to identify behavioral cues that lead to crisis, in order to intervene and prevent the crisis.

Physical Restraint

A team of Hartford Courant reporters and researchers were perhaps the first to compile a national database that listed deaths associated with the physical restraint of psychiatric in-patients[44]. The database documented 142 deaths from 1988 to 1998. Partly as a result of this knowledge, regulatory agencies began to require proper and documented procedures be followed before, during, and after restraint.

Only as a final resort after de-escalation techniques have been attempted and when there is immediate danger to the resident or those around him is physical restraint

---

[44] Weiss EM, et al. Deadly restraint: a Hartford Courant investigative report. *Hartford Courant* 1998; October 11 – 15.

employed. Formal procedures are taught to staff for minimizing the danger inherent in physical restraints.

The length of time that a resident is in a physical restraint should be minimized as well; there are techniques for carefully and gradually removing restraints once the resident is in the recovery phase.

As stated above, after recovery there is an opportunity to TATER and learn alternative choices that would not only avoid the restraint but develop new conditioned behavior.

Chapter

6

The Comprehensive Cognitive Behavioral Model

Therapeutic Resonance

*N*ow that we have reviewed elements of the cognitive behavioral approach to the resident, we shall address using it comprehensively across all treatment modalities.

The fundamentals of CBT are taught to each resident in individual and group therapy. We developed the *Think Again* workbook, previously described, as an introduction to the cognitive behavioral concepts.

Residents then use those principles in various interactions with staff, including in the school, in various groups and recreational activities, during individual and family therapy, and in interactions with nursing and with their psychiatrist.

As illustrated in the figure below, all of these interactions revolve around and support activities of daily living through the milieu.

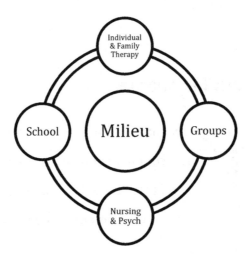

Each individual and family therapist has had formal academic training in CBT. All staff who interact with the resident were given training in CBT initially on hire, then given periodic recertification with competency re-evaluation, and was offered in-services on more specific applications for the current resident mix. Having a consistent approach to the patient by each treatment modality enhances and amplifies the overall effectiveness in a therapeutic *resonance*.

The Cognitive Behavioral Milieu

The use of this phrase is intended to refer to a residential milieu that incorporates a cognitive behavioral approach to facilitate the psychological, emotional, and behavioral growth of the residents. The cognitive behavioral milieu is coordinated by the cognitive behavioral milieu therapist (or cognitive milieu therapist, or milieu therapist).

> ### Remember:
> The idea is for the resident to be continually mindful of the cognitive behavioral model to problem solving.

There is very little literature on a cognitive or cognitive behavioral milieu. Soth [45] (1997) recognizes elements of three treatment models in the cognitive milieu: 1) a primary therapist model where the major responsibility for

---

[45] Soth, N.B. (1997), Informed treatment: milieu management in the psychiatric hospitals and residential treatment centers (p 28). Medical Library Association and The Scarecrow Press, Lanham, Md. & London.

cognitive therapy (individual, family, and group) remains with the primary therapist, with a staff educated in cognitive principles providing support; 2) an add-on model, with a cognitive aspect added to basic milieu treatment as the psychotherapeutic component; and 3) the staff model, employing cognitive behavioral therapy as the principal form of therapy. By "staff" is meant any employed individual who has an interaction with the resident as part of their job description and, therefore, is consistent with the "comprehensive" cognitive behavioral model described earlier.

Hanna[46] suggests that for acute psychiatric care all staff should be trained in CBT. Rosebert and Hall[47] detail experience with training acute care behavioral health staff to implement CBT techniques in acute patient encounters.

---

[46] Hanna, J. (2009). *Cognitive behaviour therapy for acute inpatient mental health units: working with clients, staff and the milieu* (p 11). Routledge Publishing.

[47] Rosebert, C. & Hall, C. (2009). *Cognitive behaviour therapy for acute inpatient mental health units: working with clients, staff and the milieu* (p 143). Routledge Publishing.

Wright et al.[48] discuss steps involved with the development of a cognitive milieu for acute adult inpatients and potential obstacles to its implementation. Various models are described including a Primary Therapist Model, a Staff Model, and a Comprehensive Model. An implementation timetable for the Primary Therapist Model is given as 24 weeks and that of the Comprehensive Model "several years".

The Cognitive Behavioral Milieu Therapist

A residential youth care worker's job description may vary considerably depending upon the facility, but here we define the position as an individual serving in a key position for the recovery of the residents. Responsibilities range from maintaining structure on the unit –a behavioral aspect – to integrating formal individual and group therapy into everyday responses to the environment – a cognitive aspect. This range places great demand on the milieu therapist.

---

[48] Wright, J. H., Thase, M.E., Ludgate, J.W. & Beck, A.T. (1993) The cognitive milieu: structure and process (pp 61 – 87) Chapter 3 in *Cognitive therapy with inpatients: Developing a cognitive milieu*, Wright, J. H., Thase, M.E., Beck, A.T. & Ludgate, J.W., editors, The Guilford Press, New York.

The milieu therapist should work in conjunction with the resident's individual therapist and, depending upon what stage in therapy the resident happens to be in, therapeutic "homework" assigned by the individual therapist can be illustrated by the milieu therapist within the milieu.

> ### Remember:
>
> The professional milieu therapist welcomes crisis as an opportunity for change.

However, the milieu therapist can serve the residents at any stage of their development in the principles of cognitive behavioral therapy by identifying opportunities in the milieu for exploring cognitive behavioral concepts.

The milieu therapist is not a friend per se, but more than a friend in that empathy and compassion are unconditional. Anger does not beget anger. The milieu therapist is continually interpreting each resident's behavior, comments, and body language for clues of impending crises or otherwise opportunities for cognitive interventions.

Chapter 7, *Inside the Cognitive Milieu,* further describes the concept of the cognitive milieu therapist and how that person coordinates the cognitive milieu.

Implementation of The Comprehensive Cognitive Behavioral Model

In the book *Good to Great* Collins[49] states:

> "Making the transition from good to great doesn't require a high-profile CEO, the latest technology, innovative change management, or even a fine-tuned business strategy. At the heart of those rare and truly great companies was a corporate culture that rigorously found and promoted disciplined people to think and act in a disciplined manner."

The thinking behind the idea of the adoption of a pervasive and consistent cognitive behavioral approach to the resident represents such disciplined thinking. The very idea of cognitive therapy itself is a form of disciplined thinking that we bring not only to all clinical staff but most importantly to the residents themselves.

---

[49] Collins, J.C. (2001). *Good to great: why some companies make the leap – and others don't.* Harper Business.

On October 21, 2003, Lakeland Behavioral Health System adopted a resolution to adopt and implement a system-wide comprehensive CBT model as the foundation for treatment of our residents and acute patients[50].

Key elements to facility-wide adoption of CBT as the foundation for psychotherapeutic interventions were:

- Leadership
- Training and resources
- Continuous monitoring/ evaluation
- Re-education and support

Leadership

If an organization is to make a major change in the culture of care such as this one, certainly the directives need to come from the top managerial level.

An organizational chart for implementation in our system appears below: The CEO should make it clear that this is an

---

[50] Lakeland Behavioral Health System is an acute and residential psychiatric facility mainly for children and adolescents; these concepts were presented in a meeting held in Dallas, Texas, October 20 – 22, 2003.

excellent opportunity to provide superior care for the residents and empowerment for staff.

The Director of Nursing (titled in the organizational chart below The Vice-President of Clinical Services) must assure that all current and future clinical staff receive CBT instruction - managed by the Education Department - and verify implementation of this training on the units.

The Medical Director oversaw the adoption process and developed a timeline for implementation. Approximately one year was required for the cognitive behavioral approach to be implemented Hospital wide.

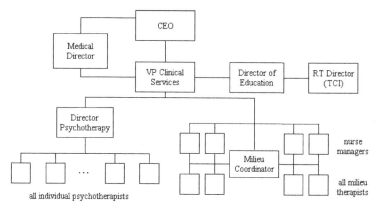

A key position was the creation of the Cognitive Milieu Coordinator. This individual was an exceptionally skilled cognitive milieu therapist. That person's responsibilities included:

- Provide CBT training to all milieu staff including didactic and on-the-unit demonstration of the cognitive techniques involved, as well as evaluation of each milieu staff for certification as a cognitive milieu therapist.
- Provision of general milieu support to staff and patients on all units.
- Be available and respond supportively to patient crises.

The Milieu Coordinator reported directly to the Director of Nursing and worked closely with the nursing supervisors and other nursing personnel on each unit.

The Director of Psychotherapy or Lead Therapist had the direct responsibility of seeing that each employed individual therapist understood the principles of CBT and implemented features of this psychotherapy in individual or group work with the residents. This leader assisted the therapists with the specifics of implementation for any particular resident. Interactions of the individual therapists with the milieu therapists was encouraged and expected. The perceived effectiveness of this approach and any suggestions for improvement was vital feedback to report to the Director of Nursing.

Each unit manager, also reporting to the Director of Nursing, ensured that CBT was implemented in his milieu, including by nursing staff. A lead milieu therapist on each unit was responsible for observing implementation in the milieu on an around-the-clock basis as well as ensuring interaction of milieu staff with the Treatment Team to facilitate the use of CBT after a resident experienced a trigger. This person also assisted the milieu coordinator in efficiently reporting current issues in the milieu.

Allied Health Professionals

The Allied Health Professionals (AHPs) were expected to learn and utilize the elements of CBT on their own. There was clinical oversight to assess whether or not each AHP was effectively incorporating this therapeutic framework into individual, family, and group therapies.

Coordination of the AHPs was assisted by the designated coordinators for the AHPs, who were also members of the Implementation Team. Senior clinical management staff also met with the AHP coordinators.

Nurses, Milieu Therapists, and School Teachers

Nurses, Milieu Therapists, and school teachers received their initial training in a four-hour seminar which included role playing and illustration of CBT principles. Clinical supervision and on-the-job training was provided for all clinical staff: for the nurses by the nurse managers; for the school teachers by the principal; for the milieu therapists by the milieu coordinator.

Each milieu therapist was required to demonstrate competency in actual situations on the unit as evaluated by the milieu coordinator. Each milieu therapist was also required to show continued use over a one-month time interval. Documentation and demonstrated communication with the treatment team or individual therapist was part of this responsibility. Proven competency was recognized with a certificate indicating that the staff member was a "cognitive milieu therapist. " Continued competency was required to maintain that title.

Group education for the residents was provided by either the individual therapists or the milieu therapist or both. This greatly facilitated the understanding by the resident of this technique and accelerated individual psychotherapy. *Think Again* workbooks were provided to the residential units for a five-session group approach to CBT. "Thought records" were utilized on the unit, facilitated by the milieu therapists for various triggers, and examined by the individual therapists. The group sessions were periodically repeated so that new residents would receive this training.

CBT Implementation Team

An Implementation Team was formed consisting of the CEO, Medical Director, Director of Nursing, Director of Psychotherapy, Milieu Coordinator, and a representative of the Allied Health Professionals (AHPs). This group provided further coordination, guidance, and oversight for CBT implementation. It met weekly during the initial stages of implementation, then less frequently as the need decreased.

Training and Resources

The Education Department initiated and required the training and competency of each current clinical staff member as well as new hires.

The training for the psychotherapists who were employees consisted of six seminar hours including clinical illustration of the techniques in action. This was a live tutorial for existing individual therapists and then subsequently provided in video format for any new hire. Successful completion of a post-didactic, written competency examination was required. Most importantly, there was subsequent observation of CBT skills with patients in therapy and required demonstration of their incorporation in therapy over two months. There was close clinical supervision by the Director of Psychotherapy during this time interval. Evidence of incorporation of CBT into the Master Treatment Plan was required. There was continuing review of competency and indication that it was an integral component to individual, family, and group therapies.

We used a series of journals published by The Change Companies[51] based on CBT principles that the residents sequentially worked on throughout their stay. These interactive workbooks were introduced at various ascending stages of treatment starting with the first journal titled *Why Am I Here?*

The *Think Again* workbook was introduced very early in treatment and the residents were required to demonstrate mastery of the concepts by passing a competency exam and discussing the principles with staff. The workbook was used both in groups and on an individual basis.

This book *The Cognitive Milieu* was written to provide overall guidance and training for the milieu therapists and was presented in segments periodically during in-services to the staff.

Continuous Monitoring and Evaluation

Monitoring followed the organizational chart. It was necessary to gain momentum quickly and maintain that momentum until there was facility-wide acceptance of the

---

[51] The Change Companies, Carson City, Nevada

approach. One objective monitoring technique was to observe the Master Treatment Plan for inclusion of CBT-oriented interventions and their completion.

Possible Obstacles to Full Implementation

CBT is a very active form of therapy requiring daily work by the resident and much direction by the therapist. The extra effort, "homework", and documentation may be considered a negative feature by some residents as well as some therapists.

Acceptance by the individual psychotherapists to utilize CBT as a predominant technique in their therapy could prove to be an obstacle. Some therapists had their own favorite therapeutic approach or wished to use techniques with less structure. If they could not see how to use CBT for a resident with a particular disorder, support and guidance was available. Allowance for selection of an alternative individual therapeutic approach needed to be considered on a case-by-case basis. For example, behavioral techniques may be quite appropriate as an adjunctive approach to treatment for lower functioning patients.

Possible confusion may occur as to the role of the individual therapist versus the milieu therapist. The only professional actually administering formal therapy with documentation of the progress was the individual therapist and this needed to be clearly explained. Therapeutic goals were established by the individual therapists and, for example, "thought records" or procedures to "rethink" triggers are assigned. The milieu therapist should be aware of these assignments and when there is a trigger for a resident, encourage their completion. Some facilitation of the assignment may be given by the milieu therapist, but interpretation and evaluation of the material is to be left to the individual therapist.

Early in the initiation of a more cognitive element to the program, some staff may feel that they will lose control over the residents. Soon after implementation, however, it will be apparent that in fact many more tools become available for them to effectively shape behaviors.

Re-education and Support

Particularly in the first few years after implementation, CBT principles and their application need to be reviewed or there may be attrition to more ad hoc approaches.

We recommend a formal review for all staff at least every six months.

The Comprehensive Cognitive Behavioral Treatment Team

If one consistent approach to the resident is to be successful, communication amongst the treating professionals is paramount. One important vehicle for this communication is the Treatment Team.

The Treatment Team is an assembly of a variety of professionals each having a unique perspective of the resident. These perspectives, once combined, allow an understanding of each resident beyond that which a single professional could achieve. Representatives of the treatment team met every morning for updates on resident behavior, and the entire Treatment Team (with the lead milieu therapist for the unit) met every other week for staffing on each resident.

Each resident had an individual therapist who assumed the main responsibility for formal CBT training and CBT homework. The attending psychiatrist was the head of the Treatment Team and coordinated the overall care of the residents. The school was represented at team meetings by one of the "team teachers". The Nurse Manager of the unit coordinated staffing materials and the reporting of the results of the Treatment Team meetings and changes in the Master Treatment Plan (MTP). The Case Manager and Recreational Therapist provided invaluable feedback and services, and the milieu therapists were represented as well.

The importance of each team member understanding the treatment goals for each resident and his particular issues and needs cannot be overstated.

Feedback Control of Treatment Planning

An important fundamental in industrial quality assurance is continuous feedback control[52]. The production of a "good widget" requires a dynamic sampling of product characteristics. These characteristics are compared to a goal and if the differences are too great, changes in the process parameters are indicated, constituting a "feedback loop".

This is what should be done in the development of a "living" MTP. The needs of the resident, first evidenced by the admission assessments of each professional discipline and summarized on the initial psychiatric evaluation are represented on the initial MTP. Regular review of the MTP and the patient's progress is an opportunity to make appropriate adjustments.

Think of the long-term goals of the MTP as an outcomes measure. Ultimate successful completion of the long-term MTP goals would then represent a good outcome. If the

---

[52] Aiken, R. C. and Wiscomb, W. (1979). A wait and see control strategy in wastewater plant control loops. ISA-79, National Conference and Exhibit, Chicago. (ISA Pub. C.I. 79-582).

---

current outcome is reviewed at each MTP staffing update and adjustments made to the plan to better reach the long-term and short-term goals, the overall final outcome is more likely to be favorable.

CBT very nicely lends itself to objective, identifiable, short-term goals and the long-term goals of self-understanding, self-control, and stronger self-esteem.

The Cognitive Milieu Therapist in Relation to the Treatment Team

In a comprehensive cognitive behavioral approach, each discipline, although quite distinct in its perspective, approaches the patient similarly, using a cognitive behavioral model.

The cognitive behavioral milieu therapist takes a unique role in that this professional helps the resident apply training presented by each of the other disciplines. This is possible because the milieu therapist is often present during group therapies, school, recreation, and spends the most clock time with the residents during a typical day.

Core Cognitive Behavioral Therapeutic Program

The following is a description of the therapeutic elements of a residential therapeutic treatment program utilizing CBT. Emphasis is placed on formal advancement of the resident's understanding, internalization, and successful practice of cognitive behavioral therapeutic principles.

There are two basic aspects to most residential treatment programs:

- Behavioral
- Psychotherapeutic

Behavioral aspect of unit program

Although these two aspects overlap, the first one, behavioral, encourages appropriate behavior through the following principles (see Chapter 2 for a discussion of each):

- Discipline
- Positive reinforcement
- Response cost

There are many approaches to utilizing these principles, all having in common offering or removing attractive privileges based on whether or not certain expected behaviors are achieved by the resident. We shall focus here on the psychotherapeutic program aspects employing CBT.

Psychotherapeutic Aspect of Unit Program

The four stages - or phases - classically adopted in CBT individual therapy are generalized here to apply to treatment objectives in the unit program. Once a certain phase has been accomplished, it is not "taken away" or "lost" regardless of behavior. Completion of the final phase (Phase 4) is meant to be associated with program completion and discharge.

In Phase 1, titled "Beginning", the patient is introduced to CBT concepts through the workbook *Think Again*. This workbook sets out the basic structure for CBT and is referenced throughout the residential stay, including in handouts that are used in the milieu to practice principles.

New residents are assisted in completing the workbook by their individual therapists as well as the milieu therapists who have been trained on how to interpret and teach the contents. Residents must complete a competency assessment before moving on to Phase 2.

Also, in order to "set the stage" initially, the residents are to complete the Change Companies journals[53] *Why am I Here?* and *I'm Okay*.

After initial case formulation, the MTP addresses problems and develops goals to be accomplished using CBT.

During Phase 2, "Understanding", the resident learns the concepts of triggers, automatic thoughts, and how they are related to feelings and behavior. The residents receive assistance in the milieu in "real time" by the milieu therapists and collect completed "trigger homework" for review by their individual therapist.

When sufficiently trained, the resident completes the full TATER sequence handouts on relevant situations as they

---

[53] The Change Companies, *Why am I Here?* and *I'm Okay* journals copyright 2000.

arise in the milieu, again with the assistance of the milieu therapist and for later review with their individual therapist.

Beliefs and values are explored by the Change Companies journals[54] "Faulty Beliefs" and "My Values".

Progress is recorded in the MTP. When the resident has shown sufficient mastery, he begins Phase 3. Elements in the MTP include satisfactory completion of the journals, demonstrated proficiency with the TATER concept, a list of typical triggers leading to unwanted emotions and/or behavior, and typical irrational or dysfunctional automatic thoughts leading from the triggers. Experiments testing irrational automatic thoughts or beliefs will be appropriate MTP therapeutic interventions during this phase.

Phase 3 is titled "Changing", and while this is the most important stage, it is not introduced until the other stages are completed. Of course, the residents are likely to begin alternative thinking on their own as they are analyzing their thoughts, feelings, and behavior - but it is not formally required until they are very familiar with their triggers,

---

[54] The Change Companies, *Faulty Beliefs* and *My Values* journals copyright 2001

their resulting automatic thoughts, and some irrational core beliefs.

Residents use worksheets from *Think Again* to help train themselves to think alternatives that are more rational and lead to improved feelings and behaviors. This is once again assisted by the milieu staff and analyzed by individual therapists.

MTP assignment goals include successful written completion of *Think Again* worksheets, demonstrating effective re-thinking of irrational automatic thoughts in response to typical triggers pertaining to problems on the MTP as well as identification of irrational core beliefs and replacement with rational ones.

After a new set of rational, positive core beliefs have been introduced to replace irrational, negative ones, the resident goes on to the fourth and final phase of treatment.

Phase 4 "Transition", prepares the residents for independent work post-discharge. They are no longer required to fill-out worksheets. Instead, they are expected to go through the CBT process in their mind, or verbally.

This is assisted by the milieu therapist and analyzed by their individual therapist. The ability to do this is demonstrated by the lack of conflict on the unit and at home during passes. They are also required to complete the Change Companies' "Moving On[55]" journal.

MTP goals include verbal demonstration of the CBT concepts employing rational core beliefs, as well as reduced emotional and behavioral conflict at school, on the unit, and at home on passes. A relapse prevention plan (or "Success Plan") is to include strong CBT elements and should be in place and understood by the residents prior to discharge.

---

[55] The Change Companies, "Moving On" journal copyright 2000

Inside the Cognitive Milieu

People are often unreasonable, irrational, and self-centered.

    Accept them anyway

The good you do today will be forgotten tomorrow.

    Do good anyway.

People really need help but may attack you if you do help them.

    Help them anyway.

Give the best you have and it will never be enough.

    Give your best anyway.

Because, you see, in the final analysis, it was never between you and them anyway[56].

*I*n this chapter we shall explore the Cognitive Milieu in action. The cases offered are an amalgam of actual

---

[56] Modified from The Paradoxical Commandments by Kent M. Keith and from the adapted version credited to Mother Teresa

encounters with residents by cognitive milieu coordinators over a five-year time interval; we shall assign the hypothetical name Jon to the milieu coordinator.

Case study: You asked for it

> *"Nothing is impossible; the word itself says*
> *"I'm possible!" ~ Audrey Hepburn*

Jon: *"I'd like to ask you a few questions to understand what it's like for you to be in the program here. I'm going to take notes and use this information to help with program development. Is that okay with you?"*

Resident: *"Yeah that's cool."*

Jon: *"First of all why were you placed in this program?"*

Resident: *"Because of my anger and depression."*

Jon: *"You were placed into residential treatment because of your emotions?"*

Resident: *"Oh, well I was getting into fights, not going to school, using drugs and stuff."*

Jon: *"Right. So what do you think about that behavior now and how are you doing here?"*

Resident: *"All that stuff was really stupid. I'm doing good here and have learned a lot."*

Jon: *"Could you give an example of something you have learned?"*

Resident: *"Everything – like I think now before I do stuff."*

Jon: *"Could you give a recent example of that?"*

Resident: *(after a little thinking) "Yeah, like last night my Dad said that he couldn't visit this weekend like he said he would – that really made me mad. I wanted to hit the wall or scream and yell or throw a chair or something but I didn't."*

Jon: *"What did you do to keep from having that kind of behavior?"*

Resident: *"I did a TATER in my head."*

Jon: *"Could you explain what you mean by that?"*

Resident: *"You know, I first identified the trigger, which was my Dad saying he couldn't visit; my automatic thought was that he didn't care enough about me to visit and that gave me a bad feeling – the emotion was that I was hurt and angry. But then I rethought about it. My Dad said that it was expensive to drive 200 miles to visit and the transmission was acting up – so maybe that is true and it wasn't because he doesn't care about me. And besides he didn't really say he was going to visit before, he just said he was thinking about it.*

Jon: *"So after this thinking how did you feel?"*

Resident: *"Well I was still disappointed but I didn't feel like hitting anything. I felt better."*

Jon: *"That was good work. How did you learn to do that?"*

Resident: *"It's CBT – we do that all the time. We have CBT workbooks, do CBT groups, use it in individual and family therapy, even in school."*

Jon: *"In school?"*

Resident: *"Yeah, like if I start to give up doing math – I don't like math – the teacher will ask me what I am thinking and I realize I am having the same old thinking that I am stupid and can't do math so I catch myself and try again. If I still can't get it, I'll ask for help."*

Jon: *"Good work. What's it like living on the unit?"*

Resident: *"Well I'd rather be home, but it's not too bad."*

Jon: *"Okay but what do you like about it and not like so much?"*

Resident: *"Too many rules and too much drama from the younger kids but I like the outings."*

Jon: *"How about the staff and the way they treat you?"*

Resident: *"Oh that's good – they help me with my problems and are there to talk with me when I want to. They help me with my MTP goals and stuff."*

Jon: *"What's one thing on your MTP?"*

Resident: *"Write down four of my core beliefs and say if they are real or not?"*

Jon: *"What are wrong core beliefs?"*

Resident: *"I think that's when you are triggered and have a thinking error, it's because of a wrong core belief."*

Jon: *"That's very good. So is there anything you would do differently if you could change the program?"*

Resident: *"Yeah – order out pizza at least once a week."*

Analysis: The resident appears well along in his program and has internalized elements of CBT and used the concepts successfully in his environment. He is likely close to discharge.

Case study: Group chaos

> *"I can't change the direction of the wind but*
>
> *I can adjust my sails to always reach my*
>
> *destination."* ~ Jimmy Dean

I knew something was going on immediately upon entering the unit when I saw Sean leaning against the wall and staring flatly into space. Nothing extraordinary in itself, but this was not the posture or affect typical for Sean. I allowed my instincts and senses to work freely as I entered deeper into the unit, noting the elevated noise level, seeing residents moving a little faster than usual to and fro.

I took report from a milieu therapist on the last shift, the morning and early afternoon one, and my suspicions were verified: the unit was escalated.

I decided to explore this with the group and asked all the residents to gather in the day area.

Jon: *"I understand that many of you have not been doing as well as usual today and I wanted to find out why so we can change that. Does anyone have any idea why things are going poorly?"*

After a pause, one resident said:

Group Member: *"I don't know about the others but it kind of sucks that I didn't get a pass to go home this weekend – some others did and we're stuck here."*

Another resident spoke up.

Group Member: *"I'm just tired of being here."*

And yet another.

Group Member: *"Yeah and it's been too loud on the unit."*

Other residents verbally agreed with these statements and began side comments to each other.

Jon: *"Okay, please quiet down and let's focus on this. So maybe some of you wish you were home and maybe the unit hasn't been a very pleasant place to be today. Right?"*

There was general agreement.

Jon: *"Let's treat this unit situation just like any other. What's the trigger?"*

Group Member: *"Being here."*

Jon: *"Not quite. It might be the thought that you'd rather be at home right now though."*

Group Members: *"What's the difference?" several suggested.*

Jon: *"A very large difference. Going home might be a goal that you are working toward but it is a fact that right at this moment you are here, and if you can't accept what is, can't accept reality – that's a problem. Being here is not the problem, it's in your processing of being here."*

Group Member: *"Okay so a trigger is the thought that I am here and I'd rather be home like some of my peers on pass".*

Jon: *"Let's start there. What is the next immediate thought that comes to mind?"*

Group Member: *"I'll never get out of here."*

Group Member: *"Nobody really wants me to be home."*

Jon: *"Those would be automatic thoughts. So how does that feel?"*

There was a consensus agreement that negative emotions were associated with that kind of thinking.

Jon: *"So I'd like to point out that the response to such negative feelings could result in a unit that is escalated. Do you see? So let's re-examine the trigger and think through this again. So the trigger was the thought that I am here and I'd rather be home like some of my peers on pass and a first thought was I'll never get out of here, for example. Let's take that one. What is an alternative thought?"*

Group Member: *"That the fact is that I am here trying to get the help I need and I know that I will be discharged once I am ready for it."*

Jon: *"Good job! And knowing that you will be discharged when it is the best thing for you, what kind of feeling do you have with that thought."*

Group Members: *"Better."*

Jon: *"Okay, so I'd like everyone to keep in mind that what you are doing in this program is quite worthwhile and will not only lead to going home but staying home and being happier and more successful. Now let's go about our day – remember we have an outing later this afternoon. Anyone who would like to talk about this more just see me after the group – okay?"*

Group Members: *"Okay."*

Analysis: Not only can individual negativity be addressed with a cognitive approach, but also group negativity. This can be particularly challenging as the negativity spreads from resident to resident and there is a group identity that exists in addition to the individual identities.

Under such conditions, a good approach can be to address the situation with the entire group. If individual members of the group are encouraged to identify the triggers and suggest alternative thinking, there can be improved group identification.

Case study: Two residents "thinking again"

"Try to be a rainbow in someone's cloud." ~
Maya Angelou

Steve: *(with basketball)* "What's going on?"

Daniel: *(sad expression)* "Nothing."

Steve: "Looks like something is going on."

Daniel: "I just failed the math test."

Steve: "Are you sure – we won't get the grades back until Monday."

Daniel: "Well I'm pretty stupid, so yeah."

Steve: "You're better than me at reading and English, so what does that make me?"

Daniel: "I think I'll just not go to school anymore."

Steve: Hey, I suck at math, too, but maybe we can figure it out together, it's still early in the term."

Daniel: "You'd do that?"

Steve: "Maybe - after I beat your butt at basketball!"

Daniel: (grabs basketball) "Think again, dude."

Analysis: Steve was perceptive of Daniel's emotional state post-trigger. Daniel's automatic thought after a tough math test was that he had failed it; his core belief was that he is "stupid". Steve encouraged Daniel to think again about how he did on the test and the reality that there was still time to improve. Steve showed empathy toward Daniel, plus he helped establish a plan to address the grade deficiency. This re-thinking plus friendship led to Daniel having a more positive emotion and overall solidified their friendship. Quite a positive outcome.

Case study: Good for good.

> *"If you change the way you look at things, the things you look at change."* ~ Wayne Dyer

Jon is at the nurses' station preparing to lead another group when Brandon was brought back to the unit from school. Jon got up and went over to Brandon.

Jon*: "What's going on?"*

Brandon*:* (angered*) "I was kicked out of school."*

Jon: *"Good."*

Brandon: (even angrier) *"I said I was kicked out - suspended."*

Jon: *"Good."*

Brandon: *"How is that good?"*

Jon: *"Well, I assume you displayed behavior that was sufficiently poor in the perception of the teacher to warrant suspension. And so, as one would expect, there was a consequence. Without the consequence the behavior might continue or worsen, disrupting the rest of the class from learning. So while your behavior might have been bad, the fact that you received an expected consequence is good."*

Brandon: (looking a little confused but less angry) *"Oh, okay."*

Analysis: As long as the rules of the unit, school, recreational therapy, etc., are well known with explicit consequences and rewards also well known, the residents will expect the rules to be enforced. They will, however, test the limits at times. Being sent out of school triggered Brandon, but his behaviors likely deserved the expected outcome. When one experiences what is expected, that can be a good thing.

Case study: Jon's diary

"If you don't change direction, you may end
up where you are heading." ~ Lao Tzu.

Dear Diary,

Today Mark got out of control and had to be
physically restrained. He jumped over the nurse's
station and started throwing files, overturning the
printer and breaking the monitor. He took a swing
at one of the nurses who was trying to calm him
down. Mark has only been here for about three
weeks but had been doing pretty well, even earlier
today before the incident.

Mark has a really tough history. His biological
father physically abused him before he left the
family when Mark was about seven years old –
he's 15 now. His mom was an addict and
neglected him; he was taken out of the home at
11 years old because of the neglect and has been
in and out of foster care since then; in one of the
foster homes he was sexually abused – I think the
perpetrator was one of the older foster kids in that
home. His current placement doesn't want him
back.

He came to us after being in acute care. He was
having frequent anger outbursts at school and
home during which he would destroy property and
strike out at his foster family and teachers –
anyone around him. He admitted to his school

counselor that he didn't care if he was alive or dead. So today's event was similar to behavior that brought him to us.

I was concerned that he might also have suicidal thinking, like before when he was having these behaviors. It was necessary to hold him for about ten long minutes during which time he was flailing his arms and legs. Then he stopped struggling and started to cry. At that point we slowly released him and I went with him to his room.

He didn't want to talk. I didn't want to leave him so I sat down on the floor in his room by the door so I could also observe the unit. We shared some time and space without conversation. I think he respected that. It took about 15 minutes before he looked at me briefly. I thought that was a cue to offer verbal support and maybe an opportunity to do some therapeutic work.

"Mark, were you injured during any of that?" No response.

"What triggered you?" Again no response.

I gave him another couple of minutes; again he looked in my direction, maybe to see if I was still there. Maybe as an opening to communication.

"Mark, I know a little about your past, you've had a rough go of it."

Mark snapped back, *"You don't know anything about me – you have no idea!"* Finally an opening for verbal communication.

"Well, I know you have had a past and that it was difficult. Right?"

Mark didn't answer verbally, but shifted his position from lying in bed to sitting upright in bed with his head down.

"And I know something else I'd like to share with you: there is no past, that's why we say it has passed." Again he didn't reject my speaking with him, although no verbal response.

"One of my favorite sayings is 'we learn from the past, prepare for the future but live in the present.' Right at this very moment there is no problem and we can deal with the now. The past is only a concept but a useful one if we learn from it."

As I said these words I thought maybe this was too philosophical and complicated for this traumatized young person. However, Mark responded.

"Oh there is a problem right now."

"What's the problem, I don't see any problem", I said.

"I just tore up the nurses' station," Mark stated slowly.

"True, and there will be consequences for that, as you know. But that's not a problem, just reality, so that's okay. It would be a lot worse if you had no consequences."

"I need a drink of water," Mark said, changing the topic and disconnecting from our conversation.

Mark got his water and wanted to rest in bed. In the meanwhile, I checked his chart and read the last progress note from individual therapy two days ago that revealed his anxiety of once again being "abandoned" without a known placement post-discharge. He wouldn't have another individual therapy for 5 days; he has no family therapy as he has no family.

As I was still concerned about possible thoughts of a destructive nature, including suicidal thoughts, I waited for an opportunity to speak with him further. I got my chance after dinner in the day room.

"Mark, mind if I chat a bit with you?"

"Okay," he said without much affect.

"So what was your trigger?"

"Everything."

"So there was nothing in particular that happened?"

"Lots of things have happened."

I was able to determine that the trigger was an internal one, namely thoughts that had to do with his perception of past and current abandonment. He stated convincingly that he was not suicidal. As I suspected, he was worried about his future placement and assumed it would be only temporary until he was again rejected.

"Remember what I said about the past? That there is no past? Well guess what, there is no future either – it doesn't exist, it's only a concept. We can prepare for it but we can't do anything now in the future."

I continued, *"So your trigger was both bad memories of the past and fear of the future and your automatic thought was rejection?"*

"Yeah, I guess."

"Would you say your behavior today helps you prepare for a positive future or not?"

"It doesn't really matter," Mark stated rather sarcastically.

"Of course it matters, you know that it does. What if we worked on improving your thinking to be more positive so that your behavior is more consistently positive? Would that maybe have a positive effect on your future?

"Maybe – could I go to the bathroom now?" Mark said after a long pause.

That was again the use of an acceptable request that ended the current sensitive conversation. I think there was an opening today that we can build upon. I charted a summary of our conversation and will speak with his therapist next opportunity.

Analysis: This was a potentially dangerous situation for the resident and those around him and needed extra attention to help stabilize the situation. It was also an opportunity for growth and learning more about the resident so as to better individualize his treatment.

The main point here is to be available to the resident while keeping watch for dangerous behavior. The exploration of his thoughts and emotions is more complex for this resident and should only be attempted by an experienced milieu therapist.

Case study: Life is difficult

> *"I'm not crazy about reality, but it's still the only place to get a decent meal."* ~ Groucho Marx

Sarah was discouraged. She didn't like "being in treatment," and the rules and expectations were not easy for her to do. School was hard. She didn't like the other kids on the unit very much. Her relationship with her parents was poor – it seemed she could never please them.

Jon: (walks up to Sarah, who is sitting down)
"Okay, Sarah, time to put things away and line up for med pass."

Sarah: *"No."*

Jon: *"No?"*

Sarah *"No."*

Jon: *"Why not?"*

Sarah: *"I'm sick of this place – I'm sick of everything."*

Jon: *"Why is that?"*

Sarah: *"It's too much – too difficult."*

Jon: *"What's difficult?"*

Sarah: *"Life – life is too difficult."*

Jon: *"Well of course life is difficult. That doesn't mean it's not worthwhile. Haven't you done things that were difficult but felt good about accomplishing them?"*

Sarah: *(no verbal response, looking the other way)*

Jon: *"Sarah, the key is accepting that life can be difficult. Then it's not so difficult."*

Sarah: *"Wha..."*

Jon: *"Just accept what is, because it is. That's reality. But go ahead and plan for improvement."*

Sarah: *(Looking at* Jon *and smiling) "You're weird."*

Jon: *(chuckling) "Maybe, but the present reality is that it is time for med pass. Let's go."*

Analysis: Many of our residents have had unpleasant experiences in their "story". But their story is not who they are. They tend to be more negative than most people their age when they enter treatment, but everyone experiences the fact that life presents many challenges (some would call them problems). Some are relatively big and some are small.

Sarah has her set of challenges and doesn't want them. Her trigger is the thought that life is difficult and she won't accept the challenges. Her automatic thought is that she is sick of everything and can't go on. As a result she is miserable.

Jon attempts to help Sarah understand that of course life can be difficult. It is difficult for everyone. If one can accept that fact, then when one comes across a challenge, large or small, it can be passively accepted as part of the life situation. Surrender for now to the now. Really it is quite illogical and unrewarding to struggle with what is, because it is. Of course one can recognize the challenge and construct a plan and begin to improve the current situation, but along the way accept what is.

Jon tries to hint at this thinking to Sarah. The concepts are simple but foreign to her. She may or may not know that what he has said is correct but it does divert her negative stream of thought and leads to a better emotion and therefore a better response.

Case study: Stop signs

> *"To improve is to change; to be perfect is to change often."* ~ *Winston Churchill*

CBT works for residents of all ages and stages of social and cognitive development, even those younger in age or developmentally delayed. We have tried modification of the TATER Think Again approach for that population, called "Stop Signs". The idea is if a resident is not following directives or is engaged in a negative activity, we go to that person and say "yellow light". If they continue the undesirable activity, we say "red light" and sequester the child from the activity, group, or whatever was the engagement at the time. We speak with the person by asking if he was going the "good way" or the "bad way."

Once he identifies that he was going the "bad way" and why, we say *"way to go"* and give him the "green light."

Red, yellow, and green cards, perhaps cut into circular shapes, can illustrate these traffic signals. We have even had the milieu coordinator dress in a full-body traffic light costume with red, yellow, and green lights that would light up from a control pad in the costume.

Here's an example of how it works:

> Billy is 11 years old and cognitively challenged. He is screaming obscenities and running down the hall away from his transition spot by his room.
>
> Jon: (looking at Billy directly in front of him with a yellow card) *"Yellow light."*
>
> Billy stops for a moment, looks at Jon and runs down the hall again yelling. Jon follows him and shows the red card "red light." Jon then sits down with Billy at the end of the hall and asks:
>
> *"Billy, were you going the good way or the bad way?"*

Billy is distracted and Jon has to ask several times before Billy says:

"Bad way."

"What was bad about that way?"

Billy: (after considerable redirection) *"I yelled."*

Jon*: "Right! What else was the bad way?"*

Billy: "I ran away."

Jon*: "Good job! Now are you ready to go the good way and sit quietly in your transition spot?"*

Billy: (nods his head yes)

Jon *"Way to go." (Billy smiles).*

Analysis: The TATER sequence is simplified by introduction of the traffic light concept - one that the patient probably is already familiar with. Red means stop and green means go. There are two ways to go: the good way and the bad way.

The more complicated part is the yellow light. It means "caution" – you are heading the "bad way." This cue can be enough for some residents to slow down and stop going that way and instead go the "good way." If not, then the resident is assisted with stopping and thinking again about which way to go, assisted by the milieu therapist.

Case study: Caught being good

"Correction does much but encouragement more." ~ Johann Wolfgang von Goethe

Sometimes we as milieu therapists are looking to stamp out fires when there is no fire – not even smoke. That lends itself to a different kind of opportunity, illustrated here.

> The unit is quiet now after quite a bit of disruption. Molly, however, stayed away from the "drama", reading her book. She is reading her book now as well.
>
> Jon: *"Molly, could I interrupt your reading for a minute?"*
>
> Molly: *"Sure, what's up?"*
>
> Jon: *"Well I noticed you stayed away from all the drama and was quietly reading your book. I want you to know I appreciate that."*
>
> Molly: *"Yeah, it kinda triggered me but I didn't want anything to do with it, so I just ignored them."*
>
> Jon: *"Well, that wasn't easy to do but you did it and I'm proud of you."*

Molly: *"Thanks!"*

Analysis: Patients who successfully completed our program were asked what we could do to further improve it. A frequent comment was:

"Give more attention to those of us who are doing well."

This is an excellent point. It is also important to give positive attention to those who often seek negative attention but are doing well currently. Such attention may be a simple compliment but could also just be engaging in a normal conversation that has no apparent overt therapeutic content. The interaction itself and the positive milieu is the message.

INDEX

AUTHOR

Richard Aiken holds a PhD from Princeton University and an MD from the University of Utah, where he also was a tenured professor. He has written numerous articles in peer reviewed journals and books. A most recent book is the *Think Again* cognitive behavioral workbook for adolescents and young adults. Dr. Aiken taught and researched at the Eidgenössische Technische Hochschule in Zürich, Switzerland, as well as the Kungliga Tekniska Högskolan in Stockholm, Sweden. He has lectured throughout the United States, Europe, and in the Middle East. His Adult Residency and Child Fellowship were at Washington University in St. Louis. He is a board certified psychiatrist and has been the Medical Director of Lakeland Behavioral Health System for 18 years.

Made in the USA
Middletown, DE
26 October 2020